SIMPLE PROCESS IMPROVEMENT

The art of process improvement
decoded into 5 simple steps

EDUARDO PEREZ

Logical Language Books

ISBN-13: 978-0-9994580-0-6

DEDICATION

This book is dedicated to my lovely wife, the person who picked up my slack as it pertains to kid & other responsibilities during this period.

Those little creatures didn't know that when dad was writing his book, they were supposed to be easier to parent.

My wife, the love of my life for the past 18 years, has never left my side and has been my biggest critic and supporter. Without her, there is no way this book would have ever come into fruition. In addition, her inputs throughout the process of developing this book were always perfectly timed. Thank you for your unwavering support and unconditional love.

This includes continuing to love me, despite dark, patchy bags under my eyes as a result of sleeping 3 hours a night for four months straight, as I did all work associated with this masterpiece. ☺

CONTENTS

ACKNOWLEDGMENTS

I thank all who in one way or another contributed to the completion of this book. First, I give thanks to God for his guidance and blessing me with the time and ability to do this.

I am also thankful to my former employers and teammates who have given me the privilege to be able to experience, learn and apply the principles I wrote about.

I am grateful to Jason Sherman for being a great supporter, business partner and mentor as well as for assisting with inputs. In addition, I give thanks to the following people who have helped me professionally via mentorship, motivation or by educating me in one way or another: Steve Thibodeau, Tyler Anderson-Lennert, Kathryn Saab, Erich Gosch, Lacie Lee, Dan Kavanaugh, Brent Godfrey, and Richard Wade.

I am very grateful to my personal friends for their continuous support from the sidelines and their genuine love for me, I couldn't ask for a better group of supporters.

Furthermore, I am thankful to my parents & my siblings who have been the biggest cheerleaders my entire life. My parents sacrificed a lot for my well-being, and for this I am eternally thankful.

Finally, I am thankful to my wife, Rosa Perez and my beautiful children, Alessandro and Natalia, for constantly encouraging me, praying for me, and showing me unconditional love.

INTRODUCTION

Have you ever found yourself with the assignment or simply the desire to make improvements, but you simply don't know how to start because things frankly appear to be running smoothly? Have you been put in an absolute do or die situation, where if you don't make the appropriate improvements to your organization or department, you may no longer have your job, or even worse, your business may not be able to survive?

You have a few options. You can choose to dive head-first into the pool of process improvement offers flashing before you on search engines and guaranteeing you success. You can opt to pay some mega-bucks to hire an external consultant, who will come to your organization and tell you how to fix things but likely will only provide you with the plan, leaving you to implement it yourself. Or you can opt to staff a process excellence department and bring on people with all the right credentials. We all know how these attempts go. You will end up paying money that may or may not actually solve the problem you were aiming for. You may end up asking yourself, "Did I really just hire someone to tell me what I already knew?"

This book is intended for new professionals who want to make a career-making impact on their businesses, small business leaders who know they have plenty of opportunities to help run their businesses better, or business professionals who are in a position where they have no option but to deliver major results. In *Simplified Process Improvement,* you will learn how to turn your business around using the proven methodology I have digested into five very easy to follow steps. You will be guided in a language that any professional at any level can understand—I gutted all the complex process jargon. No longer do you need to have an extensive background in process improvement to deliver impressive process improvement results that will be remembered for years. I have also incorporated five real-life business turnarounds that I personally led. I walk you through each case study from before it started through the final results in a manner that allows you to understand my thought process. My objective is not to impress you with ridiculously awesome turnaround stories, but rather to educate you and give you the confidence to understand that you too can deliver the same if not better results.

I wrote this book for a few reasons.
1) I wanted to share with the world the methodology I have personally used to deliver outstanding results year after year. I have been able to repeat the same level of results in various companies—ranging from small to large—in various industries, and in various types of roles.
2) I was tired of seeing companies throw away money into programs, certifications, and consultants and not get the results that were promised in the end.

3) I wanted to inspire any professional within any organization to believe that he or she can personally make a big impact. There are few opportunities better than an end-to-end process improvement turnaround to develop and display leadership.

4) Finally, I was tired of seeing process improvement professionals confused or trying to impress non–process improvement professionals with their lingo, credentials, and specialized knowledge of tools used in an exclusive community. With my approach, you will understand what they are doing and saying, since I will translate it into layman's terms. I will incorporate somewhat complex process improvement tools into this book, but it is my objective that you will not even notice them.

The material is presented to you in the format of a case study, followed by Step 1, followed by another case study, then Step 2, etc., until we reach Step 5. Each detailed case study contains each of the five steps. My objective is to give you a chance to try to decode my *Simplified Process Improvement* methodology as you learn it chapter by chapter. By the end of the book, you will have been exposed to the five simple steps and the five remarkable turnaround stories, and essentially had an opportunity to learn something and then see it in action.

To protect the privacy of the companies I worked with, specific data and details and the names of the process steps, people, departments, and companies have been slightly modified. However, the learnings, applicability, and results do not change.

Now, let's jump into one of my personal favorite turnaround stories, case study #1!

CHAPTER 1
CASE STUDY 1: *AUTOMATING THE MOST COMMON TASKS FOR EFFICIENCY GAINS*

This is a case from when I worked as a process engineer with Hotel Super Experts Corp. (HSEC). There were over 1,000 employees in the West Coast Call Center division where I was serving. For the most part, the processes were relatively consistent and functioning well. The operation was a well-oiled machine for a company that had been seeing continuous growth and was beginning to take a strategic leading position in a challenging market. Sales were increasing, the business was profitable, the call center was delivering great customer experience numbers, and the company had a great image in the travel industry.

I thought to myself, "I have essentially just been given a blank slate to work with. There are various types of projects: 1) In some, you already have a problem identified and you are told to address it; 2) in some, you are told there is an issue in a specific area we want you to focus on but don't know the specific problem; 3) in some, you are given an area with a specific motivation, as in, "We want you to help us with quality," etc.; and 4) in some (as in this case), you are told we don't know what to fix and we don't know the area for you to focus on." This was not a case where the business lacked humility and believed everything was perfect: Rather, it embraced a continuous improvement spirit and knew that even when things appear to be going swimmingly, there is always an opportunity to improve.

The Approach

Given that this was the type of effort where I actually had time to work with and was given liberty on what to focus on, I determined that, provided the West Coast Call Center had 1,000 employees, efficiency would be a good place to focus on, since small tweaks can lead to major efficiency gains. In addition, there were no existing data to work with, so I saw this as a great opportunity to meet with people on the floor and conduct an extensive time study across various sites with people at different skill levels and in different types of roles. I was going to gather my own data, however, literally the old-fashioned way: I was going to sit side-by-side with employees in the call center with a stopwatch and track how long each specific task took. My plan was to avoid making this so obvious that employees would know that I was measuring them, which could influence their behavior, in a phenomenon known as the *Hawthorne Effect*. Therefore, to track the employees' times, I utilized a stopwatch website link hidden behind a spreadsheet I was using.

At this point, I had no data, minimal knowledge of the process itself, and no specific problem to fix. In most cases, this would be scary to a process engineer. However, I was looking forward to meeting new people, becoming extremely knowledgeable about the process, and traveling to our other site.

[At the same time, I trusted my ability and was confident the disciplined approach I was taking would reveal something valuable.]

As simple as this approach is, it is still to this day one of my favorite approaches if you have adequate time to work with. You are guaranteed to learn something valuable to share with business leaders, and if you do it right, you will definitely identify a problem to solve.

When I served in this capacity with Hotel Super Experts Corp., I reported to the process engineering group, though I was assigned to and supported the West Coast Call Center. I put my proposed approach together and stated that I would need about two weeks to gather all the information I needed. In addition, I would also need a junior process engineer to come with me to help me in side-by-sides, and there would be some travel required. At this phase, it was simply data collection. I received approval from my management and my business partners. I also requested key contacts, which consisted of the business leaders of the Sacramento and Reno sites where I would be performing my time studies. I then contacted them and informed them of what I would be doing and that my efforts would have minimal impact on few employees in their call centers. We would simply sit with them and ask them about their process steps and watch (and time) them doing their work. The business leadership was aware of my motives and was very supportive.

The Data Collection

When you have large operations with hundreds of people doing the same thing in a repetitive manner, you can assume a few things:

a) If a few people are making a mistake or performing a task incorrectly, then there is a high chance the rest are doing the same thing.

b) On a similar note, people find ways to work around standard procedures if they find their own ways to do things more efficiently (than the standard procedure), and word spreads fast, leading a majority also to perform the task this special way.

c) A small tweak has a large ripple effect, which can be positive or negative.

d) There is likely a large gap between top performers and bottom performers; based on my observation, I tend to attribute that gap more to hard work and diligence than to differences in the steps performed.

I gave the instruction to my assisting process engineer that we would be spending the first day at the Reno site simply identifying the process steps (and in sequence) performed by people of similar roles. We both ended up sitting with about 10 people that day and observing each perform about 10 cycles of the same thing. That evening, we reviewed our notes and developed a basic flow of steps that the call center employees performed for each phone call they completed. There were some steps they performed prior to the call, some steps during the call, and then, depending on the outcome of the call, some steps were performed after the call. This cycle was repeated over and over. I then developed a very basic spreadsheet with the 15 or so steps on the left side, then to the right of that some spaces to document how long each step took, and then a way to identify varying paths. I provided my assisting process engineer with instructions on how to sit with employees without interfering with their work, but with the liberty to ask questions if he didn't understand what was done, and then how to track their times and take appropriate notes.

I informed the business partners of what we would be doing for the following days and asked them to give us a list of names of employees of varying abilities, including their top, middle, and bottom performers. In addition, I asked them to inform the call center employees of what we would be doing with them so they wouldn't be caught off guard.

We went off on our data-gathering journey the following day. We continued with our effort through the end of the week and then did the same at the Sacramento site.

[At the end of these two weeks, I had in my hands extremely valuable data that kicked off an effort that led to $5.5 million in savings initially and the continuation of these savings year after year in unspent costs.]

Now that I have your attention, let me jump into how I analyzed the manually obtained data and turned them into gold. After collecting the data, I divided the primary steps into buckets and turned this into what the typical day of the call center employee looks like in the form of a pie chart that represented the eight hours of paid time. With this information, I was able to communicate to leadership at both sites what our employees were spending their time on (see Day in the Life of a Call Center Employee Diagram). In addition, I created a visual of the length of time of various 'paths/scenarios' (see Various Path Time Flows).

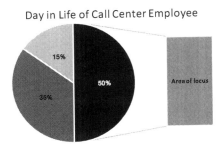

Day in Life of Call Center Employee

■ value-adding   non-value adding no opportunity   ■ non-value adding

After doing this, what I did was put my own judgement and knowledge into categorizing the process steps into one of three categories: 1) Value-Adding, 2) Non–Value-Adding with opportunity, and 3) Non–Value-Adding with no opportunity.

I categorized *value-adding activities* as those items that the business leaders and/or the customers are willing to pay for someone to do. For example, a car salesman's value-adding activity would be the act of actually selling a vehicle to a customer. *Non–value-adding with opportunities* are tasks that the business leaders and/or customers are not willing to pay for someone to do. An example of this using the same job would be paying a car salesman to do research on vehicles or using worktime to take classes to learn about the various paint colors of various carmakers. Finally, a *non–value-adding without opportunity* is an activity that a customer and/or business leader is not really willing to pay for but knows that it cannot be changed or minimized due to legal, compliance, or other inflexible reasons. In our example, this would be the time a car salesman takes to take a licensing test or the time invested to complete legal paperwork. One thing to add here is that there is often debate about what is value-adding versus non–value-adding; I used my own judgement in this project despite some business leaders' not being comfortable hearing what percentage of their employees' time is actually adding value to their bottom line.

My analysis revealed that only 35% of the work that the call center employees performed was value-adding; 50% was non–value-adding with opportunities, and 15% non–value-adding without opportunities. Generally, what you want to do once you have this information is work on maximizing value-adding activities and minimizing or eliminating non–value-adding activities. These were hard numbers to swallow, but with the strong foundations of my methodology, full documentation, and transparency in the process, my assessments carried a lot of credibility. In addition, there was a certain path/scenario that revealed that 25% of an average employee's day is spent placing calls that no one answers. What I did next was use the data to identify what areas I would be attacking to work on minimizing non–value-adding activities, leading to efficiency gains in the process.

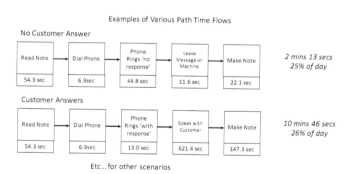

Examples of Various Path Time Flows

Etc... for other scenarios

The Analysis and the Plan to Find Solutions

After assignment of the non–value-adding activities, what I did was observe that one aspect in particular grabbed my attention. I determined that I would go for reducing to eliminating the amount of time that the call center employees spent writing notes or engaged in post-payment activities to set up payments based on a customer's preferred payment channel. Even though these activities are important and must happen, given my definition, they are still non—value-adding and should be reduced as much as possible—or ideally, employees shouldn't be doing these things at all, letting technology automate them instead. I observed that approximately 20% of an employee's day at the West Coast Call Center was spent typing notes and triggering payment activities. In essence, any reduction of this is an efficiency gain that can be applied to a 1,000-person workforce. Those efficiency gains can be applied to laterally move those employees to other open positions across the business and avoid hiring new people.

To resolve this, there were two elements that I needed to find the solution to: First would be to identify the most common notes, and second would be to solve for how to reduce or eliminate the amount of time those notes took. For this portion, what I did was continue to utilize the talented call center employees within the business to form a frontline-based team. This is one of my favorite approaches for researching and finding solutions, given that frontline personnel know the operations better than anyone else because they repeat their processes thousands of times a month. In addition, it is a way to boost morale by giving them an opportunity to be involved in a project outside of their normal daily routine.

I formed a group whose purpose was to identify the most common outcomes of calls with customers. I called this group the Purple Team. We met three times a week for three weeks. I would assign team members items to research and data to gather to come up with a solution to bring to our team. After the three-week period, we were able to propose solutions that would significantly reduce note-taking time and, in some instances, eliminate it altogether.

We learned that, approximately 70% of the time, one of three scenarios ended up being the outcome. If we addressed those three, we could significantly reduce note-taking time, and then we could even take the route of aiming to reduce the other 30% of less uniform and less simple outcomes. For the 70% group, we measured the specific steps down to the click to perform those activities and determined that they took 22 seconds on average. To summarize, three scenarios represented 70% of note-taking activities, each of which took 22 seconds to complete, and note-taking activity represented 20% of a call center employee's day across 1,000 people. The other 30% of note-taking activities was spread across 25 less simple scenarios, which on average took about two minutes each to complete.

We took a multi-pronged approach to address the two buckets of note scenarios. First, to address the three most common scenarios, we proposed something we called *Quick Clicks*. In essence, these would be command buttons easily available and strategically placed on the call center employee's main screen. Second, to address the other group of 25 less simple scenarios, what the Purpose Team and I did was propose a five-column set of dropdown boxes. Each of those columns would ask for different sets of information, and when they were filled out, the system would develop and publish a note utilizing the selected fields.

I thanked the Purpose Team for all their contributions and told them I would be using their inputs to develop the proposal I would deliver to leadership to ask for funding. Keep in mind that up to this point, the Hotel Super Experts Corp. had not spent an additional penny on us. I was confident in the proposed solution, given the well-documented and disciplined approach I took from the beginning. I ensured that I kept all business partners not only informed but also part of the solution-finding process, including people from the frontline all the way up to site leaders.

I did one final piece of assessment prior to delivering my proposal to business leadership of the Sacramento and Reno sites. I developed quick sketches of what the very simple screen modifications and automations would be and met with a tech developer who would be able to give me an estimated cost to implement. He came back and gave me a cost of $90,000 to implement the changes. With this information, I was able to develop a grounded business case, where I stated a cost of $100,000 with a conservative efficiency cost savings of $2,000,000 over the span of the first 12 months, representing a 1,900% ROI.

I scheduled the meeting with the appropriate stakeholders, and I delivered my proposal. We received approval for the tech funding and were assigned a project manager to partner with me in implementing the changes.

The Execution and the Results

Because of the expertise I had gained in the effort and the documentation I had amassed up to this point, the technical delivery was simplified. We held a kickoff meeting that consisted of the project manager, developers, and me. In this meeting, I discussed what the intent of the technical changes would be. I made sure to state my desire to place the three Quick Click buttons in highly prized real-estate space on the main screen. There was pushback, but ultimately I also sold them on the other benefits—that the notes our employees developed would be documented in a consistent manner and would lead to fewer problems downstream for all parties. In addition, developers typically like to have freedom with their design, so I was sure to communicate that I was open to the look and feel of the changes as long as they satisfied my two requirements: 1) The buttons were easily accessible on the main screen, and 2) They automated the three most common note-taking activities. Regarding the development of the five columns of dropdowns, they suggested a sixth column to account for an issue they were aware of and decided to address with this project. I had no issues with this—it is always a great feeling when you can kill two birds with one stone. Or, as technical people like to state, they may as well solve the other issue since they are already *under the hood*.

When you get to this phase, the solution normally seems relatively simple, but it is never as easy as it seems it should be from a technical perspective. One challenge in particular that we came across was in the automation of certain tasks that I wanted as part of the Quick Clicks effort: Certain permission access rights were required, and only certain frontline personnel had those rights, per the internal HSEC policy. The permission access rights were put there for a reason, but I was able to make a case to get those permission rights granted as part of the automation efforts, given that the frontline people would not actually be making those changes themselves. After receiving this approval, the tech team went forward with getting the development scheduled. The implementation from the technical side from start to finish took approximately three months, due to other conflicting projects (which is a common challenge).

We held a mini-celebration on the launch date of the changes with all the involved parties. In this phase, I am thankful for all the people who helped to make this happen, but I am not ready to fully celebrate until the results come in. Since I'm the one leading the effort, my credibility is on the line, given that I convinced several people along the way to dedicate their time, resources, and money and to believe me and my assessments. What also adds to the anticipation is that the results often take months, and in some cases, up to a year, to come through, and meanwhile you are pulled into other projects.

We were fortunate that for this effort the results were evident within two months. The Quick Clicks took a 22-second task down to a two-second task, a 91% reduction. The six-column dropdowns reduced our note-taking time from two minutes to 55 seconds, a more than 50% reduction. By the third month, the efficiency gains were apparent in our excess capacity. The end result was larger than I had conservatively forecast, and we ended up with a 9% overall efficiency gain across the entire business, leading to cost savings of $5.5 million for HSEC after the first year, savings that continue to be avoided costs year after year. Those savings were in the form of avoided new hires, as those in the previous call center roles were laterally hired into other roles. I, along with the team, was recognized for this accomplishment via various awards, and in addition, I was asked to serve as a keynote speaker for a process excellence event to talk about the effort end-to-end from idea through savings.

Recap

This effort, which led to $5.5 million in savings, started out with the idea of doing an old-fashioned time study via side-by-sides with frontline personnel. When there is time to work with and things seem to be going very well, this is the approach that I recommend. When there isn't low-lying fruit available, a thorough assessment is typically the best approach; the worst case is that you'll learn something to share with everyone in the business. There were various characters that I interacted with along the way, but what was important was to establish a level of trust and good relationships. The people I interacted with held useful information, which, when put into the right hands, is as valuable as gold.

At a high level, the phases of this effort were

1) Permission to explore
2) Planning and approval of the approach
3) Execution of a time study via side-by-sides
4) Compilation of information via sketches, data, and notes
5) Analysis of findings
6) Identification of a problem or opportunity
7) Solution gathering with the front line
8) Business case development
9) Proposal of a solution to leadership
10) Partnership with a tech group
11) Delivery of changes
12) Waiting for results
13) Celebrating the results

One final element to take note of is that the proposal of the solutions to leadership did not come until the ninth phase. Because I had already done all my homework up to this point, I was confident in the problem, I was confident in the solution, I was confident I would get support from the appropriate partners, and I was confident that I could talk about any of the details myself because I was involved in every phase.

[The upfront work allowed the delivery to go smoothly, and given the unique situation for this case, the results came in relatively quickly.]

When observed from the final cost-savings perspective, the numbers seem inconceivable, but when broken down into the simple phases, they collectively represent a beautifully simple process improvement for Hotel Super Experts Corp.

CHAPTER 2
STEP 1: *FACT AGGREGATION*

You attend a meeting with your manager, her manager, and a few co-workers. In that meeting, one of your co-workers from a different department provides everyone with colorful charts and graphs, but the same documents are displayed on the projector in front of everyone. In this meeting, your co-worker talks in detail about declining sales numbers, saying that your company had one of the worst quarters in past three years. The following day, your manager calls you into her office and tells you that she needs you to find a way to reduce costs in your department without a reduction in quality or speed of processing. You think to yourself, "Of course, as always, I am expected to do the impossible."

Another scenario: You join a new department with a new role in an area you are not remotely familiar with. All of your peers are very nice to you and they all mention how happy they are to have you on the team, especially with your great reputation. During an informal conversation in the hallway, your new manager mentions how happy he is to have you on the team. He mentions that the department you are in now is having some customer experience issues; he is just not sure what the issue is. He gives you a pat on the back and says he knows that you can get to the bottom of it. You take a swallow and respond with, "Of course." Meanwhile, you are thinking, "Is this for real? In the interview process, I didn't know I was signing up for this."

Third scenario: You are running your own business. You work 12 hours a day and hustle day in and day out. You think to yourself, "No one works harder than I do," yet your competition seems to be catching up. You feel like everything is running smoothly, you don't get complaints from customers, your sales are gradually increasing, and you've even managed to cut costs by 3% from last year. You think, "Do I even have an opportunity to improve? It seems like everything is going well."

These three scenarios are extremely common in various combinations for anyone from experienced small business professionals to junior professionals who want or need to enhance quality, reduce costs, increase speed, or improve customer experience. Process improvement is an endless cycle, and any businessperson with the mindset that everything is perfect just the way it is and there are no process improvement opportunities is in denial. Even Steven Covey called it out in his very famous book, *The 7 Habits of Highly Effective People*: the seventh habit is to 'Sharpen the Saw.' This habit pertains to the continuous improvement cycle, and in particular he refers to the 'upward spiral.' Although the book goes into detail specifically about people, the same principles apply to taking your organization through an upward spiral via continual improvement.

Back to the three scenarios. Your most likely response would be, "Where or how do I even start?" Most people do not consider themselves process improvement professionals, but I am here to tell you that as of today you are one. In fact, anybody can be one, and I will provide you with five simply laid out steps to help guide you from the point of thinking about making improvements through the point when you see and experience the results. What I have done is revisit all my past successful process improvement turnarounds like the one in Chapter 1 and analyzed the common threads in each of these turnaround stories. Despite the differences in the end goals, industries, and maturity of the processes, essentially the same basic five steps were repeated over and over for each of process improvements I led. What I will add is that I am doing my part by providing you with the five steps in a relatively simple format, but to be successful, you will require persistence, discipline, and a level of grit. What I have essentially done is use my experience to give you the formula to deliver your own awesome turnaround stories, but you will need to do your part. It doesn't matter your level of experience with process improvements, and I even propose that it doesn't matter what role you play in your organization. With the right attitude, anyone can do this.

The way I have laid out these five steps is from the perspective of what mental role you need to adopt. You will need to put on different hats for the various phases, and those different hats will require you to use different skills. Obviously, there is overlap between the various skillsets, but they are more concentrated in certain steps.

The Five Steps:
1) Fact Aggregation
2) Meticulous Planning
3) Methodical Pitch
4) Diligent Execution
5) Continuous Communications

Now, let me answer your questions on how to start.

Objective While Aggregating Facts

You are now in a position where you need to improve your process to impact speed, quality, cost, and/or customer experience. During the **Fact Aggregation** step, your primary objective is to gather as much information as possible about all the known data points, facts, theories, issues, process steps, complaints, and compliments and turn this into a process flow diagram. During this phase, resist making any assumptions, but instead approach the situation as if you were an unbiased investigator. In fact, the less you know going in, the better.

Step 1.1: Side-by-sides

Begin by scheduling side-by-sides with the personnel who perform the job on a daily basis. It is the people who perform the functions you are focusing on who know more about those processes than anyone else. Think about how many times they do the same thing over and over.

[While you may have made an observation of a certain element of the process via a chart or some data points you looked at, people on the floor have physically or digitally touched those loans, gone through the act of making something happen, and repeated this thousands of times. Trust their intuition as it pertains to the process.]

For an employee who has 100 files to work, 100 parts to build, or 100 things to process, within one month that employee has likely repeated the same actions anywhere from 500 to 4000 times. Compare this to your few observations—the point being, go to the source, since they know more than you. Treat the floor personnel with great respect and understand the value in having relationships with them. One great piece of advice from Donald Phillips's book *Lincoln on Leadership* is, "get out of the office and circulate among the troops." Our former president, known as one of the best leaders of all time, was regularly seen among the troops, and he insisted that his cabinet members do the same. He suggested that with this genuine sense of community comes trust and access to vital information that might otherwise be spread behind your back.

While you are performing the side-by-sides, don't ask leading questions. Instead, simply ask personnel how they do their jobs and have them walk you through a few examples. Ask them to tell you about issues they face and if they know about any issues they cause downstream for whatever reason. One very important thing to do is to take lots of notes during these extremely informative side-by-sides, not on a laptop but on an old-fashioned notepad. I am not mentioning the notepad approach as a personal preference, but rather as a more successful approach for gathering information, from my experience. Perform these side-by-sides with different people at different skill levels and, if applicable, with different teams and sites. Aside from approaching the side-by-sides with an inquisitive mentality, also come humbly. The more humble you are, the more comfortable your interactions will be, and the more open the employees will be to you. Once they detect pride or sense you to be a *know-it-all*, you will lose their respect, and you will no longer get honest responses or all the information you need to do your best job. My personal advice: Just be humble all the time.

Step 1.2: Data Collection

Think about the process or processes you are getting deep into and then what the various impacted metrics are. When gathering these data, do not think about them from a production perspective but from a process perspective. You must peel several layers of the onion in order to get to the core; generally, the process metrics roll up to impact the higher-level production metrics. The most common process metrics you will be looking at are the following:

a. *Speed*: How fast are the steps of the process moving from one step to the next; what is the overall time from beginning to end; how long does it take one team versus another to complete something; how long is the wait time between steps…?

b. *Quality*: How many errors are coming out of a certain step of the process; are there certain sub-elements of a process that have more errors than others; what types of error are occurring more than others and how much more; where is the work that has to be repeated regularly; what does the policy say should be happening versus what is actually happening; what are the error rates numbers; where there are mistakes how severe are some versus others in terms of cost, regulatory, and customer impact…?

c. *Cost*: What are the high-level breakdowns of costs within the process; what are the people costs of one role-type versus another; what are the material or vendor costs; are there peaks in costs at certain times…?

d. *Throughput*: How many units are produced per person; of the things that start what percentage don't make it out; is there higher throughput in certain parts of the process versus others; are there certain days, months, or teams that have higher output than others, given the same resources…?

e. *Customer Experience:* What are the primary complaints; what are the customer experience scores for various areas, days, and seasons; are there certain teams, people or parts of your process that generate more compliments than others…?

In terms of data collection, the data can come from various sources; do not discriminate against one form or another. Your goal at this point is to become a magnet for as many data as possible. Be open to data from reports, manually tracked data, data pulled from databases, and sometimes even data based on people's guesses (as in "It takes from five to seven days on average").

[The unfortunate reality is that you likely won't have perfect data available to you.]

What I call *perfect data* is having access to 100% of the data you need in a perfectly accurate form in order to perform your full assessment. Because of this truth, you may be required to gather your own data. Data collection can come from side-by-side time studies, manually looking through files and counting errors, manually reviewing customer complaints and identifying common trends, asking someone in finance to give you certain figures or giving you access so you can gather your own numbers, and so on.

During this phase, I recommend that you not go overboard with data that will not be helpful, and on the flipside, ensure you at least get what you need. There is no silver bullet on the exact right amount of data, but if you're unsure, I suggest you lean on the side of having too many data. However, keep in mind that data collection can be one of the most time-consuming stages if you aren't careful.

Step 1.3: Investigative Diligence

You have gotten your feet wet by meeting with the people who perform the job on a daily basis and have in your hands an arsenal of data; now is the time to further investigate what I call tangential process elements. These are elements that may not be as obviously based on data or what someone told you. I have developed a set of six categories for you to ensure you understand fully how they relate to the process(es) you are delving into. In addition, I have provided a few sample questions for each of the six categories to help guide you. However, the spirit of these questions is for you to dig deeper into these six categories by meeting with the right people—remember, you are not the expert.

1. *People*
   a. What do the procedures say people should be doing?
   b. If people are making errors, do they know?
   c. Is a step completed manually or automatically, or is it triggered by a different person? If so, why?
   d. Are people in the same role doing different things? Are roles clearly understood?
2. *Processes*
   a. Is the current process satisfying the business requirements?
   b. How are the inputs and outputs of the up- and downstream processes? Are they functioning satisfactorily?
   c. What are the official starting and ending points of the process? Is there any confusion?
   d. Are there any non-production processes

that impact the process being investigated?

3. *Information*

    a. Who inputs the data elements? Is it manually input, calculated, or automatically populated?

    b. Are the same data found across different parts of the process? Is there any confusion?

    c. Is it not a big deal if certain information is incorrect?

    d. Who is the source of the information provided for the process being investigated?

4. *Evidence*

    a. Are there certain notes that people need to be taking about their work as evidence of completion?

    b. Are the notes they are taking sufficient and satisfactory for the process, compliance, and data collection?

    c. Can the notes be automated? Do they have to be manual?

    d. Are there steps triggered as a result of a new note?

5. *Documents*

    a. What are the letters or documents that need to go out to the customer during this process?

    b. Are the documents up to date? Are they correct?

    c. What triggers the sending of the documents? Auto, manual, or other?

    d. Does the sending out of these documents trigger something else?

    e. What are the ramifications of a late or incorrect document?

6. *System*

    a. What are the currently known issues regarding the process being investigated?

    b. Does the system have the capability to automate certain steps?

    c. What is the interface between workers and the process being investigated?

    d. Are there multiple systems for people to interact with? If so, what are they? How many?

The sample questions underneath these six categories are simply sample questions but can be used as a starting point to help guide your thought process. The questions are not meant to represent an exhaustive list—they're just some that you could ask. The important thing to take away is to think about how these six categories interact with, make an impact on, and are part of the process being investigated.

Step 1.4: Informational Analysis

I am proud to announce to you that if you've made it to this point, you are likely one of the most informed people about the process. Most people do not take the time to do this because they are caught up doing their daily routines and performing their assigned functions. However, my hope is that, prior to this point, you have not drawn any conclusions or made any assumptions, since this would have only limited how open-minded you were to learning. Now is the time I want you to begin analyzing everything you've learned.

In this phase, you have in your hands an understanding of the process: where it is performed, what metrics are impacted, and which elements are not so obvious. Now I want you to draw conclusions, and you should begin to form an idea of what the issues are. If you were diligent enough, you may even have found the sources of some of the issues. I recommend breaking down your analysis into two portions: objective and subjective. Below, I cover some tips for developing this analysis.

1. *Objective*
   a. Using the metrics, develop charts and graphs.
   b. Show the metrics over time to establish a trend.
   c. If a timeline approach doesn't work out, you can gather data from before and after a certain point to only show two data points.
   d. Use pie charts to elucidate things that contribute more than others, such as drivers of bad quality.
   e. Be sure to label the units on all the charts.
   f. Be selective with what and how many charts you develop—sometimes less is more impactful.
   g. Finally, make your statements in terms of trends, not meeting goals or requirements, one team versus another, or certain driving issues.
2. *Subjective*
   a. Based on your side-by-sides or investigative diligence, there were likely observations such as trigger of letter extremely manual.
   b. Another example observation could be that Department X seems to be using the incorrect version of the guidelines.
   c. You will likely have to generate a long list of great observations.
   d. These observations are special nuggets that most do not have access to.
   e. I recommend splitting your observations into three to five categories and then

selecting the most important ones from each category..

f. Be sure you are able to clearly identify where in the grand scheme of the process your observations occur.

For the objective portion of informational analysis, you will need to be precise. If you came up with 22 sets of data, you will need to bring that down to 10 sets to put into charts; in a subsequent step, we will boil that down further.

[In addition, you will need to be creative. In some instances, you will notice that you know you have great data in your possession but are not sure how to present it. When you come across these situations, what I recommend is combining datasets. This sometimes turns commonly known things into powerful data.]

An example would be, you have data that show it takes on average 6.9 days to complete process step 6 and has been trending up 0.5 days the past three months. What you can do is combine these great data with data on quality. Your new chart could send a message such as, as data are trending up 0.5 days over the past three months, error rates have been increasing by 50%, and the top source of those errors is incorrect data entry, which represents 60% of the errors.

My recommendation for this phase is only to focus on the data elements that help indicate where there are opportunities to improve. Similarly, if the purpose of the process improvement is to increase process speed, then it would make sense to include metrics having to do with process speed.

Step 1.5: Develop Process Flow

The final stage of fact aggregation and your deliverable to guide you into the next stage is to develop a process flow. Do not be intimated by the sound of this. Out of everything I teach you in this book, the process flow is the only semi-technical process tool that I will call out by name. In essence, a process flow is a diagram that visually shows what happens from one step to the next. In addition, it shows that there are alternative paths in process steps, as in a decision that can lead down one path or another (see Sample Basic Process Flow below).

Sample Basic Process Flow

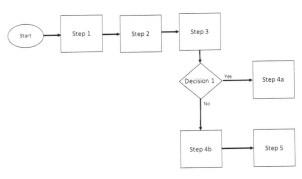

On the surface, it seems impressive, but when you break it down one step at a time, it is relatively straightforward. There are formal tools available to create process flow, or you can simply use MS PowerPoint to create it. I recommend you personally learn how to create a process flow and not have someone else create it for you. Creating your own process flow is a rewarding process during which you will ask certain questions that help educate you. Two formal programs used to create process flows are MS Visio, which is available for PC products, and Lucidchart, for Mac products. I have developed process flows using both, and I have also used PowerPoint. Some process enthusiasts would stress that certain formats should be adhered to and certain symbols should be used for specific scenarios, but I am here to tell you that if you learn these four symbols, you can map out any process (see diagram). In addition, there is no right or wrong way to create a process flow. In the end, the purpose of a process flow is to communicate information from one person to another, so if the message can be conveyed properly, you have accomplished your purpose.

Basic Process Flow Symbols

1. *Rectangle*: This is what you will use more than any other shape. It is used to contain the actual description of the step.
2. *Diamond*: This is the shape you use when you come across a decision in the process, as in, "Approved?" The response would "yes" or "no."
3. *Oval*: This stands for the end indicators—it is used to indicate the start and stop of a process.
4. *Circle*: This is usually smaller and contains a letter. This symbol is used as a reference from one point in the process flow to another. You use this to help keep your diagram neat and avoid having lines running all over the place.

Like any other skill, creating a process flow takes practice. Your skill will improve with iteration, but it is very intuitive to develop. The most difficulty you will probably face is learning how to make the program do what you want it to, be it Visio, Lucidchart, or PowerPoint.

Now that you have created your process flow, you are not quite done with this phase. With your completed process flow, what I would like you to do is to overlay your learnings from your objective and subjective informational analysis. What I mean by this is, if Step A holds the part of the process where there is a 5.4% error rate, then put this information right there on the chart. Or if Step G takes 4.3 days to complete, then indicate that right there on the chart. In addition, I would like you to overlay your subjective analysis as well. If Step E is where you observed two different methods being used across the different sites, indicate it right there. I personally like to use a bright yellow circle containing the objective and subjective analysis to make it clear what is being called out and where (see diagram below).

Example of Process Flow with Overlays

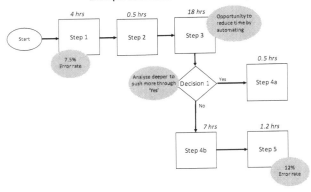

Take your time when creating your process flow, making sure to get all the parties that you met with to validate the accuracy of what you have documented. This documentation will serve a very important role in the subsequent steps.

You have now concluded Step 1 of the *Simplified Process Improvement* approach. Now, on to our next case study: This one is about the time we used manufacturing principles in a non-manufacturing environment to deliver 100% employee engagement and some other great numbers.

CHAPTER 3
CASE STUDY 2: *MANUFACTURING PRINCIPLES APPLIED TO A NON-MANUFACTURING ENVIRONMENT TO BOOST QUALITY, MORALE, AND CUSTOMER EXPERIENCE*

This is a case in which I took on a new role to lead the operations for Limited Brothers Accounting East Site (LBAES), an accounting business offering a wide range of accounting services under the umbrella company Progressive Accounting Corp. LBAES had an office we called the Processing Room that completed a lot of the paperwork for us. The Processing Room was performed approximately 30 different mini-processes, which in some cases intersected and in some cases were self-standing. These 30 processes were run by 45 different employees, two managers (Helen and Rebecca), and the office vice president, Tim, who reported directly to me. The Processing Room had been running in the same manner for years and was providing satisfactory service for Progressive Accounting, but the leadership believed that bringing a fresh set of eyes could be helpful.

When I took my initial tour of the facility, what I observed was that there were a lot of people in a relatively small space. I really liked how the place bustled with movement and energy, but I also struggled to figure out who was doing what and where things went. I provided my thoughts to Tim, who was also relatively new, and he agreed with me. This was a good sign, knowing that there would be open-mindedness toward the changes that I was thinking of at this point.

The leadership that hired me didn't make it 100% clear what specific metrics they wanted me to focus on, but after my initial tour, I made some observations. Even though the business and the Processing Room were service providers, I noticed several similarities with a traditional manufacturing environment. The available data revealed that, on a weekly basis, there were approximately 18,000 faxes that needed to be routed to a different part of the larger business, Progressive Accounting; 12,000 files needed to be pulled from shelves and delivered to various destinations; 7,500 documents needed random audits to be performed; 6,000 new files arrived, which needed to be filed appropriately; and 22,000 different files needed to be sorted, opened, imaged, and filed away in a specific manner. The similarities with manufacturing were a large quantity of repetitive activities, various processes occurring simultaneously, and the physical environment itself (as opposed to files in a server).

The Approach
What I did initially was simply take regular tours of the Processing Room. Eventually, they were no longer tours—just me walking through and talking to various people. I did this for approximately two months without changing a thing: My objective was simply to gain trust by watching

and learning. My conversations consisted of the basic question, "How are things going?" Once people become comfortable with you, it is surprising how much they are willing to share and *really* tell you how things are going. At this stage, I was simply gathering mental subjective notes via observation, and on some days, I would complete my other work while sitting in the Processing Room office. My goal was to get an authentic feel of the place: I wanted to know how conversations went, the issues and wins people experienced, and the manner in which people interacted. I was not even interested in looking at any data, even though a lot were available: I wanted to observe first, then dive into the data.

Unlike the case with Hotel Super Experts Corp., no regular check-in with leadership on status or buy-in was needed at this point. I was simply running the shop, and if I sent leadership a notification that everything was going well, no further questions would be asked. However, after those two months, my observations led me to believe that several simple changes in behavior could go a very long way.

Observations
My observations where that there was a very strong camaraderie among the staff, everyone always seemed to be helping each other out, people were flexible in working different processes when needed, and the management staff were always ready to drop what they were doing to answer any questions.

On the surface, this looks like a healthy environment, but what I observed was the following:
1) People did not have clear direction on how to address tricky situations.
2) People did not have clear line-of-sight into what work they would specifically be assigned to that

day.

3) Management did not have time to lead, since operations were highly dependent on their physical presence.
4) People often had to walk across one end of the office to the other and back.
5) Management did not know if it would be a busy week or slow week.
6) Temporary staff were hired to accommodate uncertainty in volume.
7) Even though morale seemed decent when it came to friendliness, in my conversations, people always sounded stressed.
8) The place was generally messy for the majority of the day, with the last hour spent cleaning and reorganizing.
9) There was a backlog of boxes of work literally piling up to the ceiling, and it appeared to be growing.
10) People were regularly re-doing work because of missed steps.

Even though I wasn't doing any of the actual work in the Process Room, I felt exhausted just watching the other employees. I held meetings with Rebecca, Helen, and Tim to go over my observations, and the junior managers validated my comments. In addition, they felt very uncomfortable meeting with me, indicating that they needed to return to the Processing Room to ensure things would not go awry while they were out, leading them to work late. At this point, this confirmed to me that we definitely had a problem.

Now that I had completed my subjective observations of the way things were operating, I was getting antsy to see what data I could get my hands on to either support or oppose my instincts.

Data Collection

Thankfully, some of the data I needed were readily available, but others I had to find for myself. I was flexible in the data I requested as long as they were relevant to the elements I was trying to validate. From my experience, one of the ways leaders cause projects to drag on and increase in cost is by demanding precise and perfect data.

The data revealed that employee morale for the previous year stood at 75%, which could be accepted by most standards but indicated to me that one out of every four people did not like working there. The existing capacity model that determined the number of people on staff indicated a need for 45 people, but because of unpredictability and processing delays, there was an average of 550 hours of overtime per month. This is approximately equivalent to having an additional 14 people on staff. There were a lot of other data available, but these two pieces were sufficient for I was driving at.

There were other data that were not readily available but relatively simple to gather. I wanted to know what our backlog numbers were, and I was able to obtain this by simply counting the number of boxes piling up waiting to be worked. My count, which was validated by one of the Processing Room employees, indicated we had a backlog of 150 boxes. To put this into perspective, there were approximately 200 files per box, so we had a backlog of 30,000 files waiting to be processed. This explains the feeling of always being behind.

Now, I had the data I needed as indicators of 1) employee morale, 2) costs, and 3) processing efficiency.

The Plan of Attack and Execution

The three primary data elements I would be using to measure the office's health were relatively simple to measure but would take major effort to resolve. However, from my previous experiences, I knew that topline metrics are generally all connected and move up or down together. In addition, I knew that because this was such a physical environment, there would be absolutely no wins achieved by technical system enhancements, so people were key here.

Tim, Rebecca, Helen, and I met to discuss what I was proposing, and they were not necessarily familiar with the manufacturing practices I proposed to them. I wanted them to fully understand the reasons I was recommending the changes I wanted us to make, so I took a few days to give them an overview of manufacturing practices and showed them videos of shop floors. After I showed teaching them about manufacturing practices and then shared my ideas, they actually had recommendations and provided some changes to my ideas. I really liked their new way of thinking. The main theme of our solutions was organization: organizing where people and things were located, labeling things, setting up regular routines, and organizing the way we worked together as a team.

The space we had to work with was 8,500 square feet of a physical environment containing a lot of physical files, boxes, and papers. Different things were done with those various files, and sometimes multiple things were done to the same files. To add to this complexity, multiple people did different things to various files, and sometimes there were different people working on the same file on the same day, leading to wasted time tracking down paper.

We identified a few objectives for us to address with our changes:

1) *Become a Self-Sufficient Organism:* This meant that we would get things to a state where there was not a

high level of dependency on management to function, know what to work on, and make decisions.

2) *Become Easily Navigable:* This meant we wanted to make it crystal clear where each of the processes and types of files was physically located and to enforce basic labeling.

3) *Simplify the Unboxing Process:* We knew the process of new work coming in through the back door and making its way through the room into the appropriate places had several inefficiencies and needed heavy yet simple changes.

4) *Reduce Back and Forth Movement:* We knew we had to reduce the number of steps people literally took, because the less time they spent to get from one place to another, the more time they could spend actually doing what they needed to do.

After laying out these objectives, we began to see a long list of very simple changes. We began by developing a simple drawing of the floor layout and blowing it up onto very large paper and began our brainstorming from there. The act of doing this exercise allowed us to see that we could group similar and sequential processes together. To assist with this brainstorming, we color-coded the 30 processes into seven main processes that they fit into. That color-coding allowed us to see how mixed similar processes were, and it became apparent why people would be mixed so much. What came out of this was a new floor layout. In addition, we color-coded the walls with large sheets of plotter paper for each of the seven main processes and put in large words what the sub-process was. In addition to color-coding the workstations, we also color-coded the shelves where the corresponding files would go. We then created a wall at the entrance containing all the labeled color codes on one axis and a list of all the people who worked in the office on another. We used simple magnetic circles to indicate what process(es) that person was working on that week.

To increase the sense of being able to manage the floor space visually, we added green, yellow, and red magnet strips on the corresponding shelves to indicate the age of certain files that needed work. Red indicated that the team was behind, so this was a visual trigger for management and employees that action needed to be taken.

To make it easy for employees to know what work they had to complete that day, we put five stations on five different wall spaces and installed hooks where management could hang the daily list of work for the station. People were assigned to one of the five stations, so they would go to their station and look at their list for the day. Above those lists was a tricolor flag system (red, yellow, and green). At the beginning of the day, when the manager put up the list of work, she turned the flag red, indicating that the work had not started and was ready to be started. When an employee took the work, he or she would turn the flag yellow, indicating that it was in process, and then would flip it to green when completed.

So everyone would have a better handle on the volume of work and the age of work waiting to be done, we put up some simple dry erase boards and gave them labels like 'Total Files' and 'Date of Oldest.' We had a board like this for each station, and each station had one specific person and a backup person responsible for updating the information daily. To accompany this, we set up a system where the managers would go around every day and write down those numbers in a simple spreadsheet I created.

To address the process of unboxing the piles of files reaching to the ceiling, we had one of the handymen build us three rolling wooden dividers painted red, yellow, and green. The dividers would be used to indicate boxes one week or newer (green), one to two weeks old (yellow), and then more than two weeks old (red). Initially, nearly all the 150 boxes were in the red area. In addition, we added a visual indicator showing the total count of boxes along with the age of the oldest box and made someone responsible for updating it daily.

The act of unboxing was also inefficient, but we came up with a very basic and cheap solution. We realized that there were approximately five sub-process steps in the unboxing process, but they were scattered across the floor layout. Therefore, we purchased a $100 long table and placed that table directly next to where new boxes were received. We assigned five different people to sit at that long table and work the boxes in a conveyer belt fashion, with one person handing off the work to the next. This seemingly obvious change felt ingenious at the time.

One opportunity we observed was that people had a barcode scanner attached to a desktop computer and would take a pile of files to the desktop, scan them, then return them to their original shelf. It was time-consuming for employees to walk back and forth and to find the exact shelf location. To resolve this, we developed a mobile station, so instead of bringing the files to the computer and scanner, we would now take the scanner to the files. To create these stations, we ordered two laptops, attached barcode readers via a USB connection, and purchased carts to set the laptops and files on. The solution was incredibly simple.

Finally, to tie all this together, we established a daily morning meeting that took no longer than 15 minutes. In this meeting, everyone stood up together, we would go over our numbers for the day, and any outstanding questions would be addressed. Work was assigned, and managers stated that they would be available to assist but made it clear that all the information they needed to do their work had been laid out. Those morning stand-up meetings ended up becoming fun, and the team really enjoyed them, ending them with a random chant followed by a clap.

The Results

Even though we spent several hours in the planning, brainstorming, printing, cutting, and taping phase, we only spent about $500 on the entire transformation of the place. We all came in on weekends for about three weeks straight to make the changes that we envisioned prior to full implementation. The results ended up being more impressive than we imagined they would be. It took about two months for the employees to become accustomed to the new way of working. The first subjective observation of improvement was that the managers had much more free time, which they used to continue to make things better and work on other critical projects that had been delayed.

Our objective results really became apparent at about the six- to seven-month mark, after the results came in from our follow-up employee morale survey. Employee morale came in at a staggering 100%. The new positive energy and happiness were not only shown in the survey results but in people's smiles and willingness to help each other out rather than relying on the management. Engagement scores of 100% for teams of 40+ people are extremely uncommon, so there was definitely something different here. Discussions with employees revealed that the reason for this increase in happiness came from the sense of organization, the trust they were given with their work, the ownership they felt they had, and their feeling that management was really trying to make things better for them.

Our backlog numbers, which stood at 150 boxes, dropped by 91% to 10 to 15 on any given day, which was approximately how many new boxes came in per week. All the boxes were in the green area. There were no more boxes stacked to the ceiling, and people were proud to show that the oldest boxes were only one or two days old. The team ended up becoming self-motivated and setting up their own internal goals of getting to same-day processing of boxes.

Moreover, when it came to efficiency gains, every one of the processes improved. Some specific improvements were
    1) The Green Team Fax Process moved from 13,000 to 24,000 per person per month.
    2) Remuneration Filing Process went from 11,000 to 13,000 files per person per month.
    3) QA Processing improved from 11,500 to 18,500 files per person per month.
    4) Settlement Queue Completions went from 8,900 to 19,500 per person per month.

    Combining all the efficiency improvements, there was an overall efficiency gain of 25%, leading to savings of $545,000 per year. These savings came in the form of utilizing 11 employees in other parts of Progressive Accounting. There was also a reduction in overtime by 80%, from 550 hours per month to 110 hours per month. The reason it wasn't completely eliminated was random spikes in certain seasons. The combination of the efficiency gains and the reduction in overtime allowed us to switch from a temporary employee model to a full-time-only model. In the process, we hired a few of our productive temporary staff as full-time employees, which also contributed to our healthy employee morale.

Recap

This turnaround from utilizing manufacturing principles in a non-manufacturing environment led to some extremely noteworthy results. What made this this turnaround so remarkable is that it was relatively cheap, it was a team effort, and it was simply fun to do. One additional thing to note here is a core principle I believe in, which is that even though all these processes had to do with accounting, one did not have to be an expert in accounting to drive these improvements. With an employee morale of 100%, $550,000 in savings, a 91% reduction in backlog, and an 80% reduction in overtime, one may be led to believe that the fixes were complex. On the contrary, they were simple process improvement principles that are applicable to any environment in any industry and can be performed by anyone.

The results were impressive, but at the end of this venture, what I was most proud of was the growth I saw in the manager, the happiness and energy that were reinjected into employees, and the fact that we built a system that will outlast most people who work there. We built a self-sustaining organism upon simple principles. One of the most rewarding elements of a process improvement is walking away knowing you left a lasting impression with sustainable results.

CHAPTER 4
STEP 2: *METICULOUS PLANNING*

As was observed in the previous case, there was intensive aggregation of facts prior to moving forward. That data aggregation served as the solid foundation for thoroughly understanding where the process stood.

[A mistake often made is believing you know the cause of a problem and jumping to resolve it immediately. Without aggregation of all the facts, you may miss a very important connection and not solve the entire issue, or even worse, you may have misunderstood what the issue was and not solve anything.]

Step 2 of the *Simplified Process Improvement* approach is for you to put on your detailed planning master hat. You will dig deep inside yourself and show yourself and others your ability to be strategic. Of all the five simple steps, this step is my personal favorite because, now that you've become incredibly educated about various angles of the process, you get a chance to think things through. For the most part, the other steps are task-driven and are about charging forward, whereas in this step you envision, design, and create what the future could look like based on information that very few people knew up to this point. You are essentially the architect of the operations, so this is the stage where your process improvement effort is most at risk if you don't put adequate effort into proper planning.

During meticulous planning, you must be thorough and thoughtful, understand the company's objectives, and be a strategic visionary. As Collins identifies in his book, *Good to Great,* companies that end up becoming 'great' base their strategies on understanding rather than bravado. Now that you have a great understanding of your business, build the process strategy around it—don't go aiming high at an arbitrary target and rally around that. Be the one who not only has put thought into an awesome strategy but knows how to make that plan logical and easy to understand and follow. The plan may not necessarily be easy to execute, but it should at least be easy to understand.

The specific type of planning and strategy that you develop for a process improvement is different from typical strategic thinking for the overall company in that, in this case, you are extremely focused on the process at hand along with all its upstream and downstream tentacles. In addition, you are laser-focused on the positive impacts that the process at hand can have to add value to the business rather than become a hindrance to prosperity. Be disciplined in this portion; invest the right amount of time and effort in delivering an outstanding plan. I have broken down the detailed planning portion, Step 2, into five sub-steps.

Step 2.1: Fact Reviewing Session

This is a very important session that I hold for an entire day. I don't make it longer, and I don't make it shorter. The meeting could be held with as few as two people up to as many people as you deem relevant. However, I don't recommend more than five people—I like to limit this meeting to the people who will be highly engaged with the process improvement effort and/or are extremely knowledgeable about the process. In addition, because you will be requiring eight uninterrupted hours from whoever is invited, the less impact to the business, the better.

You will hear me say this often, but I want to reemphasize that you as the leader of the process improvement need to take ownership to another level. Regardless of what title you hold (high or low), you must demonstrate leadership and commit yourself to this improvement effort. This is not for the faint of heart. As Willink states in his book *Extreme Ownership*, "the leader bears full responsibility for explaining the strategic mission, developing the tactics, and securing the training and resources to enable the team to properly and successfully execute."

Prior to the fact reviewing session, develop an agenda for the meeting, and be sure to set aside approximately four of your eight hours to simply reviewing the process flow and all the relevant data that you completed in Step 1. I recommend that this be the first thing you do in your meeting. A lesson I've learned from running these meetings is to establish some guidelines for the meeting at the beginning. Do not allow people in the meeting to have their laptops open, and ask people to be respectful with their phone use. To sidestep any need or excuse for people to be on their electronic devices, I suggest you print out all the material for people to have in front of them for reference and to take notes on. This 'threat' of no email-checking for eight hours will be very difficult for people to commit to, sadly. Unfortunately, this is the working environment of today. In my article "5 Ways to Focus in a Distracting World," way #1 is Intentionally Disconnecting; in that section I mention, "Emails, texts, social media, news, and various escalations have found a way to enter our lives and take over. If you are not prepared and haven't properly armed your ship, it will be sunk by a barrage of distracting information coming from various sources" (the article link is found in the bibliography). For this meeting, I am protecting you from distractions by not allowing laptops for one day.

Aside from the four-hour block set aside in the agenda for reviewing the process flow and information, set two or three hours aside for discussion on identification of issues that came out of your thorough review of the data and process. The issues you have identified need to be targeted down to the specific pain points. Think with surgical precision. For example, a surgeon will not say you have a problem with your left leg; instead, he will state that you have an issue with the inner part of your medial patellofemoral ligament. Issues are to be identified with this specificity, as the purpose of this meeting is to peel down several layers of the onion until you get to the core. Don't settle for general issue identification. If the group focuses appropriately and has a valuable discussion, it should almost seem obvious what the issues are. Spend the last one or two hours beginning to document what some solutions could be. I don't recommend going really deep into solutioning yet because that will be Step 2.2, but at this point, be open to people ideas and get people thoughts.

One note to add is, during this session, be sure to take

notes. You can take them or someone else in the meeting can take the role of note-taker. Regarding what else to prepare for the meeting. I highly recommend you print out, as large as possible, a physical copy of the process flow for everyone to stand up and look at together. However, please still include a smaller version for attendees in their meeting package of documents. In addition to the physical copy, if your business has the capability, you should put the process flow up on a projector. Other documents to include in the attendee document package are all the data elements, charts, and information you gathered in Step 1. In terms of running the meeting, remember you are leading the effort, so take ownership of facilitating. It is likely that people will not know how to move forward without you guiding them along. The people in the room with you definitely want what is best for your business, but you need to run the meeting in an organized way to be able to pull that valuable information from them.

If you feel like some portions are going too fast, slow things down and be prepared to ask probing questions; if things seem to be moving slowly, then be sure to remind people of the agenda and move things forward.

[For the leader of this process improvement effort, nothing beats being extremely organized and having thought out through various scenarios.]

The output of this meeting will be a set of problems or issues identified and documented along with potentially new learnings, in addition to the beginnings of solutions in the form of ideas. You and the team will likely be exhausted after this meeting, but it is one of your most important meetings in the entire process improvement cycle, so you should all leave with a sense of accomplishment because you made major progress towards the end-goal.

Step 2.2: Solutioning Sessions

Now that you have had your extensive fact reviewing session and identified all the issues and a few ideas for solutions, you can focus on identifying fixes. For this, I recommend you utilize several shorter, focused sessions. The sessions are to be held with people in various roles, with very targeted purposes. If you identify an issue with great specificity, the solution-finding with the right people should be straightforward.

Up to this point, the process improvement efforts have been almost scientific, with set guidelines and principles. Solutioning is more of an art. You will learn that there could be several solutions that you and your co-workers come up with to solve the issues you have identified. For example, let's say the issue is that processors are having to do rework and the reason is that the files they are receiving from the file auditors are regularly missing the numbers that appear before a street address.

   a. One solution could be to systemically not allow file auditors to pass the file along to the next step unless that number field is present in the system file.
   b. Another solution could be to retrain file auditors to ensure they know how to properly populate the address field.
   c. And finally, a third solution could be that file auditors don't even input the address into the system, instead having it scanned and uploaded using special technology before the file is even accepted into the system.

I could go on with more solutions, but I believe you get the point. Put on your thinking cap during this process, and be sure to consider all factors when solutioning. In some cases, you may want to consider the less expensive solution, and in some cases, you may only allow things that prevent an error from even happening. Be very attentive to what the people you work with say as you meet with them, and make educated decisions considering the additional information you have in your back pocket.

The types of roles of people you will likely meet with during the solutioning phase include your IT/systems technology people, operations team leads, frontline operations personnel, and other process SMEs. If you are not satisfied with a proposed solution, keep digging deeper. I guarantee you there is always a solution. If we put a person on the moon, how much easier is it to ensure that the numbers appear before an address field? Don't become discouraged. This should be one of the most fun parts of the whole process improvement experience.

The solutioning phase could take a few days to a few weeks to a few months, depending on the size of the effort, the number of issues identified, and the pace you are able to work at. If you realize that you have identified more issues than can reasonably be solved, then using your own judgement, rank them and focus on the ones with the most impact on what you are trying to solve. You should have the data to support your judgement at this point. For example, if you are trying to decide whether to prioritize the issue of underwriters doing extensive rework, leading to three extra days of processing, or the fact that customer experience numbers are 20% lower when you place calls after 5:00 PM, go back to the purpose of your process improvement. If your effort was about efficiency, I would lean on first solving the issue with underwriters. I would add that at this stage, if possible, I would suggest not to reduce the number of issues you are aiming to resolve yet; there will be a few other stages when that reduction may occur.

Finally, as you come up with solutions to the identified issues, be sure not to lose track of your objectives. As you develop solutions, concurrently indicate the goals your solutions would impact. For example, if your issue was that processors at your east site have a glitch on their system not allowing them to send to West Coast customers after four, which is leading to a one-day delay, and your solution was to upgrade the system and purchase the time zone patch—then tie this solution to speed, cycle-time, or whatever you named your objective.

Step 2.3: Timeline and Cost Validations

Once you have come up with solutions to the list of issues identified, you will have a set of strong, well-understood solutions that have been vetted with your various partners. In Step 2.3, your primary objective is to get timelines and cost estimates, when applicable. Everything will have some form of timeline associated with it, but not all items will incur costs.

In some cases, the business partners who provided you with solutions in Step 2.2 are the same people who will be implementing them, but in other cases, they different people will be responsible for implementation. In Step 2.2, you were simply coming up with the great ideas that you and your co-workers believed would be the best resolutions; now is when you go the extra step and determine if something will take one week or six months to implement. In addition, this is when you figure out if your great idea will cost nothing or $800,000 to implement.

Most likely, for system solutions, you will be meeting with

technical product managers; for vendor solutions with vendor managers; for procedural changes with operations managers; for training changes with training staff, or maybe you can do the training; and so on. This is another great opportunity for you to demonstrate ownership by implementing whatever solutions make sense, depending on your role and skillset and the company culture.

One more point to add is that you will likely alternate between Steps 2.2 and 2.3. You may determine that a particular solution would take too long or be too expensive to implement. If this occurs, you will need to go back to the drawing board and come up with new solutions. The good news is that, because you have already done the appropriate research, you can revisit it later in the event that leadership prefers a more bulletproof solution despite its taking longer and/or being more expensive.

Step 2.4: Multiview Plans

Now is the time for you to put together your plans that will ultimately drive the outcome of the project. The reason I call this portion Multiview Plans is that you will be creating not just one plan but a series of plans for different audiences and serving different purposes. In this planning phase, you will think through several details and place them into documents, which will likely become the documentation that will be shared and represent the process improvement itself, at least until the results are achieved.

[People who see only this likely do not know about all the upfront work you have already invested to get to this point, but that is OK. That upfront work is what gives your plan its deserved credibility.]

When putting your plans down on paper, take pride in your work and put time into making it look nice. I have witnessed some good plans not get their deserved consideration because they simply did not look professional or had distracting formatting. The content was solid, but the poor presentation on paper was diverting attention away from the valuable content.

My standard set of multiview plans includes the following, in most cases in this order:

1. *Methodology*: A few pages explaining the methodology you have utilized up to this point, which led you to the plans you are developing.

2. *Executive Summary:* This document should be placed towards the front of the package you are putting together, but I suggest you not put it together until you have thought through and developed all the other documents and plans. This should be kept to one page and only include imperative information. I've had several of these meetings when we didn't go beyond this page. That is OK—don't stress and feel like everything else is wasted work. This plan is for you to deliver your awesome results. Great planning will make your life easier in the subsequent steps.

3. *Big Blocks*: A one-page view using three or four blocks containing some form of categorization of your solutions.

4. *Timeline*: A one-page high-level timeline view of the entire implementation.

5. *Resources Needed*: Then is where you state what you need to make this happen. Do not be bashful when asking for the right tools, the time of certain personnel, or any other resources. With appropriate thought, you should be able to state

something like, "I will need 25% of Person X's time for three months."

6. *Risk Planning:* A great process improvement leader should also have the ability to sniff out any risks that could impact the success of the project. Don't be shy when identifying risks—risks are not a sign of weakness, but rather your ability to forecast them is a sign of leadership. Then, you should accompany those risks with how you plan to mitigate them.

7. *Business Case and Benefits:* I will address this in Step 2.5.

8. *Supporting Data:* As many pages as needed containing all your supporting data and charts.

9. *Communication Plan:* A well-thought-out plan on how often you will be providing updates and to whom and identifying any check-in meetings, approval sessions, recurring meetings, etc. In the communication plan, be sure to include what the item is, who will own the delivery of that item, the frequency, and what form that communication will come in (email, meeting, call, document, etc.).

10. *Double-Click Details:* A few pages containing a few levels of details below the three or four blocks. This will primarily be used by your team, but have it available in case you're asked.

11. *Daily Routine:* This may be difficult to do, but I highly suggest you go down to the detail of thinking through what your daily routine will look like for the duration of the process improvement project. If you will only be dedicating two hours a day, then indicate this and specify what you will be doing with those two hours.

12. *Process Flows:* There should be no additional work here because you have already created these. However, please ensure that they are presentable and consistent in style with the rest of the

document.

Double-Click on Executive Summary

In this executive summary,

- At the top, write two or three sentences that include the goals you are trying to accomplish with the process improvement and a little bit about the work that has already been done.
- Next, give a bullet point view of the big block items of your solutions.
- One bullet should contain the timeline from beginning to end.
- Third to last, include risks you have identified. I would not include the mitigation items at this point.
- Second to last, include the benefits and business case findings at a high level.
- Finally, your last sections should make it crystal clear what it is you are asking for. This last part should say something like: *Approval needed for 50% of X resource's time, $75,000 for tech resources, and to proceed with the project.*

The documents you are putting together beginning with #8 (Supporting Data) are the type of documents that normally come in the end and sometimes even as appendix items. They may not be as important to leadership personnel, depending on their leadership style, but those documents are probably some of the most important ones for you and the delivery team.

The entire plan should flow smoothly from one section to the next. For the titles of your slides, instead of simply naming the content, try summarizing a major takeaway for the audience.

[Allow the titles alone to tell your story. If someone were to only read the titles, would he or she be able to get the gist of your plan?]

For example, instead of calling a slide "Timeline," try, "We will be able to deliver the project in five months, and 50% will be completed by March." Or instead of writing the title of a slide as "Resources Needed," try, "Having a dedicated reporting analyst for 50% would decrease our delivery timeframe by two months." I hope it is obvious how much more compelling and attention-grabbing the titles are.

Step 2.5: Business Case and Benefits

The final portion of Step 2 is focused on your business case. In the previous section, you reserved a spot for your business case, but because this requires an additional level of thought, I wanted to go into it in further detail. By this stage, you are already extremely well informed about your issues and solutions and have lots of great plans. This part is what can make or break your entire process improvement project. However, if you have made smart decisions along the way, you should be ending with a scenario in which whatever investment you are suggesting has clear benefits.

To develop a well-thought-out business case, always begin with costs. In Step 2.3, we went through performing cost validations. You should already know the costs of the items you are planning on implementing. You have the freedom to present several different business cases or one large business case. What I mean is, you can come up with business cases broken down for different sections (one for efficiency solutions, one for quality solutions, etc.). It is up to you or your business's standard procedures whether to handle people's time as a form of investment; I generally do not calculate people's time as a cost because the company is already paying for its employees' time.

After you have come up with costs, aggregate the benefits portion into dollars. Be sure to include the benefits even for the items that do not cost anything because they are definitely still contributing to the bottom line: Those are bonus items. In an ideal process improvement, you would get maximum benefit with $0 investment. When calculating benefits as part of the business case calculations, be sure you understand the finances correctly. You will probably need to engage with someone from your finance department to give you more precise costs—for example, for savings on personnel, if this is one of the benefits you are claiming.

Your final business case should yield something like this:
- Investment (Cost): $75,000
- Return (Benefit): $100,000
- Time to realize benefit: 1.5 years

Your business case statement could look something like this: "We will yield a 133% ROI (return on investment) with a payback period of 1.5 years."

In addition, there will likely be benefits that do not yield any monetary value to the business. For these items, you should create a separate page to clearly differentiate the two. A benefit without dollar savings is not necessarily a deal-killer. Keep in mind that there are certain things that you have no choice but to do as a business. For example, if your business is struggling to meet a regulatory requirement, you may have no choice but to resolve the issue. Or if you have low customer experience scores and this is something you are focusing on as a goal, then there may be no immediate dollar benefit in increasing the scores. I don't recommend making a stretch in terms of calculating dollar benefits for customer experience in the form of increased business, because that is all theoretical. I would instead simply state that your project could increase customer experience scores from 65% to 80% based on your analysis if X items are implemented.

After you complete your business case, include it in your overall strategy and planning document. You have now completed the most thought-intensive exercise of your process improvement effort. Now, on to the next case study! This one is a great example of a process improvement effort with low dollar benefits but ultra-high regulatory compliance benefits.

CHAPTER 5
CASE STUDY 3: *CREATING TRANSPARENCY OF PERTINENT INFORMATION FOR QUICK RESPONSE TO QUALITY ISSUES*

The following case involves my team of consultants for Grey Square Consulting Group, who were hired by Natural Oil Loan Experts (NOLE) to assist with compliance with one of their loan processing requirements. In the scenario, the customer knew exactly what he needed resolved, as opposed to some of the other cases, in which the issue was unknown or unclear. NOLE provides loans for mid-sized businesses in the oil industry for prospecting, drilling, and refining. NOLE was struggling to meet one specific directive, the 25-day decision regulatory requirement, which required them to decide whether to decline, approve, or counteroffer applicants' loans in 25 days or fewer. The company was struggling so much that in the previous year's audit, an audit finding was identified and labeled as high-risk. Items with this distinction carry a risk of leading to regulatory fines, which could cause negative publicity. This was definitely an issue that needed to be resolved. There were several parties and departments involved in the loan decision process, which added to the complexity. The primary parties included sales, document gatherers (DGs), customer communicators (CCs), and underwriters (UWs); there were, however, some other ancillary processes that were involved in specific scenarios.

Background Information

NOLE processed approximately 800 loans per month, and operations was composed of approximately 30 sales personnel, 40 DGs, 30 CCs, and 20 UWs. The compliance numbers revealed that they were consistently averaging approximately 30 loans per month that were beyond the 25-day requirement, leading to a failed compliance rate of 3.8%. In some months, there were as many as 100 loan decisions beyond the 25-day requirement. The average time to decide on a loan was 19.5 days.

A loan decision consisted of any of the following:

1) A formal *approval* notice sent to the customer in written form. The date the notice was sent was used as the end-date indicator.

2) A formal *decline* notice sent to the customer in written form. It had to contain the reason for the denial as well as some other particular elements to be considered an 'official' denial. The date the notice was sent was used as the end-date indicator.

3) A formal *counteroffer* notice sent to the customer in written form. A counteroffer document consisted of a decline notice along with an approval notice. The decline notice was for the customer's requested terms, and the approval notice consisted of approved alternative terms. The

same decline requirements applied to a counteroffer decision letter.

Now, what started the clock was the point at which a customer indicated interest in a loan and began the application process. The regulatory requirement did not indicate that a completed application started the clock, which was a form of confusion initially; we will touch on that later.

On the surface, this seems like a straightforward requirement: The applicant applies, and you should provide them with a decision in 25 days or fewer. It should be as simple as taking their numbers, putting them through a decision model, and providing that decision back.

Simplified Version of 25-Day Decision Process Flow

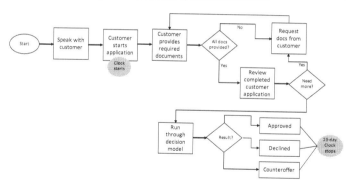

However, there were several factors and other laws that contributed to the difficulty and motivations at play.

Here is a common example of a scenario that makes abiding by this regulation difficult: A customer initiates an application but doesn't provide all the required and requested documentation. From the business side, you want to approve as many loans as possible. Simply declining is not a good option—what if the customer could be approved? So you don't want to decline the application because it may mean lost business, but you cannot approve it either because you don't have enough information to determine if it meets approval requirements. In addition, there are laws that prevent the company from simply declining the customer for not responding to documentation requests. In these situations, NOLE is required to first provide an official notice to the customer that if no response or required documentation are provided within 10 days, he or she will be declined for his or her lack of responsiveness.

The Approach

I, along with the other consultants from Grey Square, began by getting a fully grounded understanding of the legal requirements. Our objective was to establish a baseline understanding for everyone in the business to agree on and clearly understand. After we had a solid foundational understanding of the requirements, we were going to gather data on the known loan applications that did not meet the 25-day requirement. The outcome of the data collection on the known failures would be for us to peel back several layers of the onion and discover what was driving those delays. We would then focus on resolving those issues and incorporating elements into the process to prevent those errors from reoccurring. We would follow this up by identifying the right metrics to help us track the true status and age of any given loan. We would use these data to develop leading indicating triggers and reporting. This was the game plan heading into the effort.

Sample of Leading Indicator Report

Decision Age of Loan

	0-15 days	16-22 days	22-25 days	26+ days
# Loans	57	12	3	1
Color	Green	Yellow	Red	Black
Action Plan	Safe	Employee & team manager notified of loan at risk	Escalate to department manager	Escalated to vice president

The benefit of with this particular Grey Square Consulting Group team was that it was assembled to address this specific concern. The team consisted of an attorney familiar with the requirements (Saul), an experienced underwriter (Yori), a sales process expert (Uma), someone with experience in document gathering (Gregory), and the team leader (me). Knowing that this effort would require intense diligence and no interruptions, I made a request of NOLE to dedicate a meeting room to us, and rather than having formal desks, we were going to meet and work in that room together. We received approval for the room. Prior to beginning this turnaround, which eventually delivered on zero loans going beyond the 25-day requirement for seven months straight, I held one week of training on simple process improvement methods for everyone to think about, gave a detailed overview of the operations from a process perspective, and provided the team with tips on which business partners to go to for what. This pre-kickoff week was critical in that it set the baseline for the group and served as a form of motivational catapult.

Understanding Guidelines

We each were provided with a printout of the regulatory requirements that applied to this situation. We spent approximately three weeks with Saul going over the requirements line by line over the projector. Saul's expertise was invaluable, in that he not only understood the regulations' intent and spirit but also had peer contacts at other companies who could help us understand how they had addressed certain things. After this very painful and tedious three-week overview, we all believed we understood the requirements extremely well. We used this knowledge to convert the formal legal jargon into simple English that was easy for anyone in the business to understand.

After overlaying these requirements onto our business practices, we observed that several people in the business believed the requirements meant something else. One item in particular revolved around what started the 25-day clock. Sales leadership had an understanding that the 25-day clock did not start until an application was completed, but some of the CC and UW leadership knew that it was when an application was started. So it was clear that the business had a misunderstanding right from the get-go. Another misunderstanding was in what scenarios a decline could be made if the customer had not provided the requested documentation, and how many days they had until they could provide that decline. There was an additional misunderstanding as to whether the end date that stopped the 25-day requirement was based on the date on the decision notice, the date printed, the date sent, or the date received. The official requirement indicated the date the document was sent, but the printed date on the decision document was previously used. In an ideal situation, the date on the document, print date, and sent date would all be the same, but this was not the case: Due to the way printing queues ran, it depended on the time of day it was triggered, and then the delivery methods had their own ways of tracking it. To add to this complexity, some customers opted in to electronic delivery, while others preferred to receive paper mail. For those situations when the customer preferred electronic delivery, the document date, print date, and sent date were all the same, but for postal mail, they could be different. We identified this nuance and made it clear for the business to understand.

Next, we delved into the existing data of known failures. In the process of reviewing these failures, we also came up with things that may not have failed but could fail because of process vulnerabilities. We came up with four common drivers of delays:

1) Sales personnel were holding on to loans too long and not handing them off to the document gatherers and customer communicators to kick off the subsequent phase.

2) We identified an anomaly where if DGs or CCs put the loan into a particular status called Postpone Callback, the loans would fall into a *black hole*. Everyone would lose track of them until it was too late.

3) There was a process in place that required all loans indicated as declined to go through an additional review process. Because they were not officially declined in the system until the additional review was completed, no decline notice would be triggered for the customer.

4) The final and probably most important driver of delays was so simple it did not get the right attention: The age of the un-decided loans wasn't visible, and the existing reporting was inaccurate.

After we had identified the drivers of our issues, we went into solution-finding mode. We approached the issues two-fold. First, how do we stop the bleeding, and second, how do we prevent it from happening again.

To address the sales personnel issue, we had Uma hold side-by-sides with the sales partners to explain to them what we had observed and how we could work together to resolve it. Uma revealed there were a few reasons: First, the sales folks were not fully aware of the regulation—

some were, and some were not. Second, some that did know of the regulation believed the 25-day clock didn't start until after an application was completed. Finally, the third reason was a system glitch where it appeared submitted but didn't actually get handed off to the appropriate DGs and CCs. We quickly resolved the first two misunderstandings by educating the existing employees, incorporating the correct information into the onboarding process and their annual certification. We put a request in to the tech to resolve the system transition glitch that we identified.

To prevent future delays in handoffs from sales to DGs/CCs, we established a reporting indicator. This reporting indicator would hold a report with three basic colors; any loans that had begun the application process but had not been submitted within three days were shown in the green bucket, those not submitted in three to six days were in the yellow bucket, and finally those not submitted after seven-plus days were in the red bucket. These indicators had a little more bite to them than simple reports. We wanted to ensure that the sales folks were motivated to work with their customers quickly to make follow-up calls and obtain the required documentation. We create an escalation process where sales personnel with any yellow-colored loans were sent a notification with their manager copied with the specific loan numbers. Then, once loans reached red status, that same salesperson and the manager were copied in an email to the head of sales. In addition to these quickly implemented changes, we also put in a technical request to have any loans that were still in the sales queue after seven days automatically pushed to the appropriate DGs/CCs. These technical changes took about six months to implement, but by the time they were implemented, the issues had been resolved via the escalation process.

It was relatively simple to address the issue of what I described as loans falling into a black hole. What essentially was happening was that any loans that were assigned the loan status of 'postpone callback' fell off CCs' and everyone else's queue. This led to no one following up on these customers proactively; that follow-up would only occur when the CCs specifically remembered to follow up or a customer called in. The reason that CCs would use this status code was that the customer had specifically asked us not to call due to a vacation or some other reason. Once we had identified the approximate 40 loans with this status, we were sure to address them immediately. In order to prevent this from happening again, we removed this as a status altogether. We also performed a complete review of all statuses that were available and removed a few others that didn't make sense. We followed this up with the appropriate training.

Having 100% of declined loans go through an additional review process seemed like a great idea at inception. The thought-process was, "Just in case the first underwriter missed something, let's do a double-check to ensure that if a customer should be approved, he or she will get that approval from the second underwriter." However, our data suggested that this added on average four days to the cycle time due to an increase in workload and lack of pipeline management. In addition, after we probed deeper into the data, we learned that even though the additional review process had been implemented eight months ago, there had never been a decline overturn. From this we learned that we had been increasing the cycle time (and cost) for a practice that was meant to increase quality, but there had been no such quality improvement. We recommended elimination of the additional review process to underwriting management. They agreed with the proposal and put a plan in place to phase out that practice.

What we believed to be our most impactful improvement came from the implementation of a leading indicator escalation process. We developed an automated report monitored by Yori from our consulting team. The report color-coded all loans as green status if they were aged 0–15 days, yellow status if 15–22 days, and red status if 23+ days. Yori would research any loans in yellow status and send them to the underwriting managers to address. Ninety-five percent of yellow status loans were addressed prior to their reaching red status, but any loans that reached red status would be escalated to the underwriting director to be addressed immediately. In a few cases, we had loans in red status that were on day 25, and I personally had to go to the underwriting director's desk and ask him to respond to Yori's email. After a few iterations of this, he understood the process and instructed the managers reporting to him not to permit anything to go beyond yellow status. In addition, he began to incorporate the 25-Day Report, as we called it, into his daily meetings. Eventually, the discipline became a part of life, and everyone came to understand the importance of doing anything in their control to prevent anything from even getting close to red status. Yori was in daily interactions with underwriters and underwriting managers for about five months until there were good behaviors in place. Eventually, Yori handed off management and monitoring of the 25-Day Report to a dedicated underwriting manager.

The Results

The outcome of these laser-focused efforts on one specific regulatory requirement led to one of the better turnaround stories for NOLE. An issue that had been a thorn in their side for years essentially disappeared. It became such a non-issue that people forgot about it. Though an average of 30 loans per month had gone beyond the 25-day decision regulatory requirement for years, there had not been a single occurrence beyond the 25-day requirement for nine months straight, and then it fell off everyone's radar. The average time to decide on a loan decreased from 19.5 days to 13.5 days per loan, a 40% reduction in processing time per decision. Most importantly, in the follow-up from the previous year's audit, auditors and regulators were thoroughly impressed, and the business passed the audit.

Recap

Sometimes one element of your process has tentacles that extend beyond what is evident on the surface. Quick fixes for processes that fall into this bucket typically do not work. The Grey Square Consulting Group decided to take a thorough approach, beginning with the wording of the regulatory requirements, continuing on to carefully dissecting and addressing any known issues with a preventative stance, and finally providing a leading indicator report to permanently address the issue. The 25-day decision regulatory requirements became an issue of the past. The major learning was that this framework for addressing any hard-to-solve regulatory issues works.

The framework was as follows:
1) Track down the requirement.
2) Translate the requirement into layman's terms.
3) Understand the requirement.
4) Deeply understand the current state of the data/findings.
5) Identify all failures.
6) Identify anything that may not have failed but could.
7) Address known issues.
8) Put measures in place to prevent known and potential issues.
9) Put reporting in place with color-coded escalation steps as leading indicators.

CHAPTER 6
STEP 3: *METHODICAL PITCH*

You have now done extensive ground-level research, developed a great visual display of the process, identified all your issues, and developed a thorough plan for how your project will be executed, so now you're at Step 3: Methodical Pitch. The reason it is called Methodical Pitch is that there is a formula for approaching the pitch, and if you approach it in this methodical manner, you increase your chances of getting the buy-in you need. And you are looking for more than just buy-in: You want your audience to be your supporters and fans in the sidelines cheering you on. In many cases, your business may already have budgeted sufficient funds for you to deliver in the process improvement, but this does not diminish the need to hold this session.

You will accomplish these four things by taking the time to do this right:

1. *Credibility:* You will build credibility in your business as the person who is thorough in his or her approach to solving problems. In addition, you will enhance your credibility as someone who is a new subject-matter expert in the processes you dove deep into.

2. *Influence:* You get a chance to practice, test, and enhance your persuasiveness. Be prepared to be challenged, but with the right methods, which I will be covering with you, I believe you can learn to become an influential presenter.

3. *Resources:* You will get to an opportunity to lock in the resources you need to deliver the great process improvements you are about to implement. Don't aim low—you may get more than you ask for.

4. *Calling Your Shot:* A few weeks or months down the road, when your project leads to stellar results, you could reference this meeting with your leadership personnel where you 'called your shot,' meaning you followed through on what you said you would do. This is not an ego thing; rather, its purpose is to build management's confidence in you so they will trust you with future similar opportunities.

Even if it is difficult for you to get formal time on the calendar with your leadership, I urge you to insist on holding this session. Why would you let up on the opportunity to accomplish the four things stated above? You have already invested several weeks to get to this point, so don't underestimate the importance of this.

There are five sub-steps that I will cover for Step 3 of the five simple steps to *Simplified Process Improvement.*

Step 3.1: Time on the Books

This may seem like a trivial step, but sometimes it is overlooked. In addition, this is about more than simply scheduling the meeting with the appropriate people.

First, identify who the primary stakeholders and decision-makers are. I would try to limit it to no more than four or five people other than you. The more people in the room, the harder the dynamic of the room/meeting will be to get through. In addition, the people you invite may decide to invite others, so keep a buffer in case that happens. If they do decide to invite others, consider this a sign of interest— a good sign.

Step 3.1 does not simply consist of scheduling the meeting and moving on—there is some preparation even for this. You have probably noticed that preparation is a recurring theme in this book.

[Be the most prepared person in every situation, and you will notice that things begin to fall into place for you over time.]

The upfront preparation I am referring to here is to think through and then develop the agenda to be included in the invitation to the meeting. Don't be overly aggressive in terms of what you plan on covering in the meeting. In the agenda, I suggest you cover a) Methodology, b) Executive Summary, c) Big Blocks, and d) Business Case. If things go smoothly, you may cover all these items and more. Keep things open and be prepared for more to be covered. In addition, be prepared for material to be addressed out of the order you had in mind. In some cases, as mentioned earlier, depending on how deep the leadership personnel choose to go, you may not get past the executive summary. The key is to be mentally prepared for things to go in various directions. Since you are the one who put together the material, you should *know your stuff*, and this should not be an issue.

Now, in the invitation include the purpose of the meeting, the agenda, and a copy of the executive summary. Add in the body of the invitation that if the invitee would like further documentation prior to the meeting, he or she should reach out to you directly. It is a very good sign if the invitee asks for more information: It demonstrates interest. I suggest aiming for a one-hour meeting; if you are unable to get this, then settle for no less than 30 minutes.

Step 3.2: Pre-Meeting Informal Discussions

At this point, the invitations have been sent, including the agenda, the purpose of the meeting, and your one-page executive summary. You can work at whatever pace works for you, depending on how much time you have prior to the meeting. During this pre-meeting period, get your attendees mentally prepared for the meeting and yourself prepared for any potential kinks they may throw into your formal meeting.

You already know who they are, so individually, in the hallway, at their office, at their desk, or in a break room, mention to them briefly that you are excited to present your process improvement plan to them. They may or may not know this meeting is coming up, but after doing this, you are on their radar. Your goal is for them to be mentally ready for you and to feel comfortable with you. In Jack Shafer's book *The Like Switch*, he covers that the "friendship formula consists of proximity + frequency + duration + intensity." The purpose of bringing these leaders to your side is so they will support you formally in front of others, and if they are aware of any potential issues with your plan, they will let you know before your meeting. You can adjust and prepare your plan accordingly and, if possible, return to these individuals prior to the formal meeting. The goal is, when you hold the formal meeting, everyone in the room will not only agree with you but also support you because their ideas have been incorporated into the plan. Leaders really appreciate being in the loop on things prior to being asked in front of others and, on the other side, really dislike being caught off guard.

Repeat this cycle to the best of your ability with all the individuals who will be attending your formal meeting. If you are unable to come into physical contact with these individuals, as a second resort, you can shoot them an informal one- to two-line email. I do not suggest simply replying to the invitation with this one- to two-line email; instead, send a separate, new email. Replies to invitations have a way of getting lost in the shuffle of emails or ignored, in my experience (confession: I personally do the same).

Again, the objective of your pre-meeting information discussions is to get a pre-read on your audience as well as to elicit informal support.

Step 3.3: Prepare Your Pitch Strategy

You now know the individuals you will be meeting with for your formal meeting; the focus now is on preparing a strategy to make use of your precious time with them. You may be thinking, "I already prepared the material and sent out the agenda. Why don't I just follow the agenda?" That is the typical way of thinking for people who deliver typical results, but I want you to aim much higher than typical. Aim to be not only the best at gathering information and developing a plan but also the best person to persuade an audience to support your plan. As John Wooden states regarding *industriousness* in his book *Coach Wooden's Pyramid of Success*, "Success travels in the company of very hard work. There is no trick, no easy way."

In the course of educating you on how to properly prepare for your pitch, I will take a little bit of a detour to the nerdy side and into the makeup of the human brain. In my article (the link is provided in the bibliography) *My Secret to Getting Buy-In—Become the Master of Attention*, I cover that the three parts of the human brain are your a) reptilian brain, b) limbic brain, and c) neocortex. You need to see that getting buy-in is a journey through your audience's brains. Your goal is to land in the neocortex, but you must first pass through the reptilian and then limbic brains, in that order.

The structure of your presentation should be as follows:
1) Stimulate a form of excitement (either fear, happiness, or a sense of urgency—basically, surface-level emotions).
2) Stimulate some form of social status and relational connection that moves beyond surface-level feelings.
3) Go into more logical and rational things such as numbers and decision-making.

If you jump the gun and try to go straight into numbers, you will lose people's attention, and they will be turned off. The key is to get attention, hold attention, and then get your buy-in. Now, to apply this wisdom to your preparation for the pitch, do the following:

Plan how you will get their attention
Think about the process's current situation and how much worse it could get if not resolved. Think about worst-case scenarios. For example, if your current end-to-end processing time is 14 days, you can state that your competitors are averaging 11 days and continuing to

shorten their days, so if we don't resolve this now, we will become obsolete. This will definitely get people's attention. Or if the situation is not this dire, you can think of another attention-grabber. Think about an upside attention-grabber. You can state that if we invest in what I am about to present, our customers will likely switch to us from our top competitors because of X reason. You know your project best; think of a clever way to do the following to your audience: excite them, make them fearful about something, bring them happiness with an interesting project-related experience you had, or provide them with something that is threatening the business. An important key here is not yet to throw out any numbers. You don't want them to try to do any calculations or try to prove or disprove you—simply get their attention.

Plan a way to hold everyone's attention
What I mean by this part is still not to put any numbers out there but rather to think of the most enticing elements of your methodology. Below is a potential flow:

a. Think of a personal experience you had with someone on the floor as you did a side-by-side. Mention that person's name as if you were telling a story to your audience. Use a similar strategy to explain other parts of your methodology.

b. Then you can get into the executive summary. Here, think of the most creative or interesting solution that you are proposing to the group. Think of a way to structure your words in a story-like manner. For example: *I met with Tom, the IT product manager. We were discussing his thoughts, and he came up with this great idea. He suggested we add a button on the top part of our system screen. We vetted out this idea and believe that we can get it delivered in a relatively short timeframe and that it will get us awesome results.* Observe how this flowed sequentially in a seemingly conversational format, and pay special attention to the fact that I did not indicate how short the timeframe is or what the benefits will be. You want your audience to be salivating for you to give them the numbers. If they begin pushing for them, remember this is your meeting, and it may take some guts from you, but refrain from providing them yet. Tell them respectfully to hold on and that you will provide that shortly.

Plan how you will drive your message home and get buy-in
If you've done everything correctly up to this point, you have excited your audience, and they are drooling for you to provide them with numbers, business case figures, and benefits. This part should come out smoothly. Since you have made your journey through their minds, the logical parts of their brains have your full attention and are receptive to what you are asking for, so be sure to state this clearly.

In this planning portion, you have prepared the strategy for your pitch. Now, on to delivering it in the actual meeting.

Step 3.4: Deliver Your Pitch

All the work related to your big meeting up to this point has been preparation and setting the stage for success. Now is when the rubber meets the road. On the day of your presentation, make sure you have printouts for everyone invited to the meeting. In addition, print about three or four extra copies in the event your invitees asked others to attend or in case they want to take extra copies with them. For this very important meeting, I suggest you not try to do the meeting using a projector. Instead, refer to the documents in front of them, and don't have them follow with their laptops. You don't want any distractions in the form of technological glitches, emails, or attempts to multitask. Consider this time like gold—you must maximize this opportunity, and you can't afford to lose it. You need all the attention to be on you and the words that are coming out of your mouth and your audience to feel what you want them to.

For your pitch, it is just as important to stimulate feelings as to stimulate thinking. In fact, I would prefer if the majority of their interactions with you are via feelings rather than thinking. If you have their full attention and execute what you planned in Step 3.3, the only time they begin to think is when you start giving them numbers.

As you proceed through what you planned in Step 3.3, be prepared for interruptions and questions. Consider this your time, so you need to control the frame of the conversation. These people are used to running their own meetings, but you will need to take control of them for 10–15 minutes. I would suggest you aim for the bulk of your planned pitch to only take 10–15 minutes and the rest of the meeting to be left to open dialogue and questions. Let them drive the meeting from there, and be prepared for questions coming from different angles.

However, remember that in Step 3.2 you already met with the majority or all these folks prior to the meeting, so at this point, this should be nothing totally new for them. Don't focus so much on the material in front of them; instead, aim for engagement, interest, and discussion.

[Even though these people are generally higher-level people, they are still human beings at the end of the day. Like you and me, they too want to be inspired, want something exciting, want to be part of something greater than themselves,

and have a sense of pride when they see people in their organization demonstrate great skill.]

The entirety of your pitch should be about the interests and benefits for the business and for those leaders in the room—it is never about you. Be selective about the words you use and frame your statements in the form of *us*, *we*, and *the business*. As Dale Carnegie says in his classic book *How to Win Friends & Influence People*, "Of course, you are interested in what you want. But no one else is. The rest of us are just like you: We are interested in what we want."

Basic Tips:
- Any time attention is diverted from what you are focusing on during your initial 10–15-minute pitch, respectfully and cleverly take back that attention.
- When asking for resources, do not appear needy. State your case with precision and step away, leaving them wanting more from you.
- Demonstrate a balance between professionalism and down-to-earth approachability. You want them to let their guard down with you.
- If at any point you compliment your audience, ensure you are genuine. When you are not, it is obvious, and it could backfire on you.
- When discussing your methodology, upfront work, or work during delivery, be sure to talk with words like *we* rather than *I*. Even though you will likely be the one who does the majority of the work, a great leader always brings those above him up.
- At the end of your pitch, genuinely thank them for their time.

The floor is yours.

Step 3.5: Post Meeting Follow Up

After you have delivered an awesome pitch and put your amazing plan into the hands of decision-makers, you can relax a little now. You should be proud that you have made it to this point. From my experience, you have just completed most of the hard work.

Take a few minutes to close the loop with these leaders. You can take the same strategy as in Step 3.2 with informal discussions, and/or you can send an email communication to the entire group again thanking them and restating what was discussed in the meeting, and if any decisions were made, make that clear. If there is an open decision left to be made, make that clear as well. Indicate that you will follow up with X Person on Y date. Remember, things will not move forward unless you drive them. Ensure there is closure and agreement to move forward; try to not to wait more than a week to get all the approvals or changes to your plans that you need.

[Freshness is important, and you want to keep the momentum moving forward. There are people counting on you—all those people who you made believe that you could drive change.]

Even though nothing has been implemented, nothing has been improved, and you have yet to witness any great results, the most important foundational work has been completed. You have essentially laid out a playbook for success. Think about it like a piece of furniture that you need to assemble. You generally have instructions with drawings showing you step by step how to put it together. The engineers, designers, and manufacturers put a lot of thought into ensuring that all the right pieces were there, that the specifications of the materials were correct, and that there is a level of confidence that if you follow the instructions correctly, you will have in your hands a pretty nice piece of furniture. You have essentially done all that work, except you cannot stop yet: Unlike in the example above, you don't just represent the engineers, designers, and manufacturers, but also the customer who will put the furniture together. The next case is a great example of doing a lot of that upfront work, followed by meticulous execution of the plan. Check it out!

CHAPTER 7
CASE STUDY 4: *ORGANIZATION OF DATA AND SIMPLE REPORTING AUTOMATION FOR AMAZING QUALITY*

This case is about a role I took as Head of Food Standards Compliance and Quality for Lactose Ice Cream Corporation (LICC). LICC was a manufacturer of ice cream products and the primary manufacturer for five of the top 10 best-known ice cream brands available in most stores. In this new role, I was to oversee the last part of the operations: the quality team and the regulatory standards reporting team. This case has to do with a turnaround story for the regulatory standards reporting team. This team had a long set of responsibilities to ensure we met industry standards, FDA standards, and corporate customer standards. We developed reporting regarding our compliance to ingredient ratio requirements for our various customers, FDA sanitary standards, compliance validation for organic versus non-organic requirements, as well as abidance by OSHA standards.

My manager, senior director of all operations, indicated to me that one of my top priorities in the new position was to improve the quality of reporting coming out of the regulatory standards reporting team. Our corporate customers commonly complained that the numbers we reported to them were often late and incorrect. Our corporate customers essentially did their own reporting on their end to validate our numbers, and most of the time, the data elements did not match up. In addition, our monthly FDA sanitary reporting was extremely error-prone, and our FDA relationship manager's scorecard for our business's sanitary reporting was red for five months straight due to data elements being incorrect, insufficient, and late, and on top of this, data were being input incorrectly into the Sanitary Reporting Standards System (SRSS).

The focus for this turnaround effort was not a case of poor operations or poor quality of our manufacturing processes but rather the low quality of the reporting to our external corporate customers and to government agencies. The FDA wrote a letter to our business president stating that if we did not get our sanitary reporting in good shape, we could face fines.

This case is interesting because even when production operations are running smoothly and with acceptable quality, if the message (via reporting) to customers and government agencies is otherwise, that becomes the perception. In addition, the regulatory standards reporting team (RSRT) was a group that, when operating well, was never noticed, but when not operating well received a great deal of attention.

Background Information

There were two basic sets of reporting the team was responsible for. The first was corporate customer reporting, which was primarily about ensuring we met their ingredient requirements. The second was government reporting, which was to ensure we met sanitary standards and that reporting was input into the SRSS platform.

The regulatory standards reporting team consisted of three personnel: David, the manager of the group; Marcus, an untrained reporting analyst; and Miller, who was responsible for general reporting and data entry into SRSS. Initially, the RSRT had a poor reputation with our customers, the FDA relationship managers, and even within LICC. The team generated 49 corporate customer reports per month, giving 500,000 opportunities for errors with the various data points reported on across all reports. In May 2012, corporate customer reporting errors hit an all-time high of 13,628 errors, but the average number of errors prior to the improvement efforts was an average of 3,425 errors per month, which represented a 0.70% error rate.

The FDA reporting only consisted of two reports. However, the data preparation prior to input into SRSS was extremely complex and took approximately 25 hours each month to complete. To give an idea of the complexity, the reporting analyst utilized 36 different spreadsheets from data sources across the company to gather the required information for input into SRSS. Aside from the inefficiency of the reporting, the FDA reporting generated 113 errors per month per our SRSS feedback loop.

I personally did not know much about this highly specialized type of reporting, had never been a reporting analyst, and also had never managed a reporting team. So, after spending about three weeks to gather this contextual information on the department, I knew this would be a challenge.

The Approach
What made this effort extra complex was that we needed to continue to do our monthly reporting, but I knew what I was thinking of would demand lots of time. After my initial three weeks of side-by-sides with the team, with the upstream (data-providing) partners, with our corporate customer account managers, and with our FDA relationship managers, I developed rough-draft process maps of the two primary processes within the RSRT.

I scheduled a mandatory full-day meeting with David, Marcus, and Miller. I prepared substantially for the meeting and developed a deck of material to go over with the team. What I planned to go over with them in the turnaround kickoff meeting was as follows:

1. Overview of the team and summary of our reports.
2. Our current error rates
3. How much time we spent to prep, develop, deliver, and fix errors each month
4. Process maps of the processes
5. Motivational staggered goals and rewards for the team

In this session, I spent about a quarter of the time going over my prepared material. They were very grateful for the time I spent digging into their processes prior to our meeting, but I indicated that we had only skimmed the surface. I used the remainder of the time to have them pull out all the data they had from their charts, data sources, and error findings. What we did next set the stage for all the improvements that followed.

We first focused on corporate customer reporting. We ended up generating a list of all our errors by bucket and then sorted them from most frequent to least frequent. The outcome was as expected: There were a few error types that drove the majority of the errors. The top three drivers of errors were 1) Blank Reason Code, with 1,126 errors per month; 2) Illogical Code Combination, with 176 errors per month; and 3) Blank Status, with 142 errors per month.

For FDA reporting, I drove us in a different direction. I wanted us to focus on efficiency, because my instinct was that poor efficiency was driving the errors. Those 25 hours per month prepping data were extremely taxing on the team, and based on the process map I developed, I have no idea how they managed to execute this every month. In the back of my mind, I was thinking that the success of this process was extremely reliant on the tribal knowledge of the team, and if any of them left the company, we would be in trouble; this was not sustainable. We used the time to identify each of the 36 sources of data and drew a large map on the whiteboard of where they were located, either digitally or physically with a department. In addition, we used color codes to identify which sources were manual, which came directly from the system, which were derived from a combination, and which were reliant on their tribal knowledge. The FDA reporting process had been around for approximately three years and was 100% manual at this point. What we learned was that of the 36 data sources, 1) 25 were directly from the system but spread out across different department systems, 2) seven were manual spreadsheets that some people tracked and then provided to Marcus, 3) two were a combination of the system and manual spreadsheets, and 4) two were based on tribal knowledge.

We ended the meeting with some goals and an action plan. The goals that we agreed upon as a team were as follows:

1) Corporate customer reporting had an error goal of 200 or fewer per month, which signified a 90% error-rate reduction.
2) FDA reporting had an error rate goal of 30 or fewer per month, which signified a 45% error-rate reduction.
3) In addition, I set out a bold goal of getting FDA reporting timing from 25 hours per month to less than two hours per month. This meant a 92% reduction in time.

When delivering the action plan, I communicated that I liked how they worked as a team, and I wanted them to continue to do this; however, I wanted them to have ownership for the various reports. In the process, David and Miller would be fully responsible for corporate customer reporting, and Marcus would be fully responsible for FDA reporting. For the action plan, I assigned different objectives to the various team members:

A) David: He was responsible for addressing the top 10 errors one at a time, starting with the biggest drivers first. I commented to him that there was no other way around this, so he needed to target each issue head-on individually, which would feel like 10 different projects. Each issue would require him to get out in the field and work with various people to resolve.

B) Miller: He would need to go into high gear during our improvement phase and be fully responsible for keeping the boat floating while David was focusing on fixing issues. In addition, I put Miller in charge of partnering with me to develop some visual tracking tools that we would be using, and I made him responsible for maintaining them.

C) Marcus: I set an objective for him to self-learn SQL in fast track mode using a book we would purchase for him. SQL is Structured Query Language, a database and reporting language. His other objective would be to develop data tables to hold all the data instead of using spreadsheets. Part of that work would include doing groundwork with each data provider and partner to help get those data into data tables rather than spreadsheets.

D) Me: I was going to document our plan and communicate with leadership so they could provide funding for the rewards I had set for the staggered goals. In addition, I designed a visual display structure for the team, and I organized daily meetings to discuss the project. Some of those elements included error rate tracking of top issues, time spent to generate FDA reporting, overall error rates, project status indicators for the various projects running concurrently, and finally, my motivational comments of support.

I made sure to really drive the point home that I was in this mission along with them to help with problem-solving, analyzing data, interpreting information, or making someone available to meet with them. At this point, they had a plan and no barriers.

The Execution

The entirety of the effort, from kickoff meeting through getting to a point of calling the effort a success, took about seven months. There were late nights, early mornings, me pulling them out of meetings so they could refocus, tough discussions with leadership convincing them that results would come, daily morning meetings around our RSRT tracking board, several process maps and sub-process maps on boards, and a lot of frustration.

It took David about three months to address our number-one error, Blank Reason Code. To solve this issue, we had to peel back about six layers of the onion. We learned that the driver of Blank Reason Code was tied to a blank field, which was tied to a field not mapping right due to an incorrect system version, and we learned that we had the incorrect system version because our technical system managers didn't know there were multiple versions. We ended up setting up a separate process to ensure our technical system managers validated the correct version for all systems. During this problem-solving phase, David would regularly come to me and say that these things were not his responsibility—my response was always that, regardless, he had to take ownership of the solution. After a few iterations of this, I witnessed David transform into a leader, and then he began telling others that he would help them out with their processes that he knew were driving errors far downstream.

After the resolution of the Blank Reason Code errors, we met our first goal on our goal tracker by hitting 1000 or fewer errors. We celebrated the first-level goal with a pizza party and cake. I was as excited as the team was because I saw a switch occur in them. They got a boost in confidence in their own ability to solve their own problems, providing the injection of positive energy they needed because they had been getting heat for their error rates for years now.

As Marcus was self-training on SQL, he began to learn about database structure and asked for certain software to do what he needed. I had to pull a lot of strings to make it happen because his role traditionally did not have the level of access he requested. Marcus ended up becoming very knowledgeable in the processes he was reporting on because he ended up meeting regularly with all the data source providers. Eventually, he would even be sought out by some business partners to answer questions about certain processes far outside his space. One of the most remarkable stories here is that Marcus, someone without a college degree, eventually became an SQL guru, so much so that our most talented business analysts within the business would go to him for advice on how to create certain queries. In addition, our database administrators would go to him for help understanding the layout of the business from the database structure perspective. After six months of hard work and 160 hours of documented effort, Marcus transformed the FDA reporting into something incredible. He developed 50 data tables to reference the 36 data sources. Like David, he worked closely with business partners to come up with solutions to their reasons for manual tracking. In addition, he developed 155 unique SQL queries from scratch to automate the arranging, rearranging, and restructuring of the data into the FDA reporting format to make it go easily into RSRT.

Miller, whose responsibly was to keep the ship afloat while David and Marcus problem-solved, also learned to lead. He led the daily meetings and in those meetings was able to provide input to the team on problems he saw, then served as a quick feedback loop for solutions that did not fix problems. He communicated data on error rates and then stood in for David in meetings when David was problem-solving.

The Results

The seven-month journey, which started off a disaster, turned a team that had a bad reputation into an asset for the business. A quote from one of our FDA relationship managers was, "These are the accounts without errors. Good news is you have no errors—What? Data must be bad. Actually, I am so happy to say this. Thanks for all your hard work." Our corporate customer partners began to comment on the quicker responses from RSRT, and our internal business partners would utilize members of the team to answer data, process, and system questions. Now to the data. Our corporate customer reporting, where we set a bold goal of 200 or fewer errors per month, ended up averaging 60 per month, representing a 0.012% error rate—1.2 errors every 10,000. This represented a 98% reduction in error rate. Our FDA reporting, where we set a goal of 30 or fewer errors per month, ended up averaging 13 errors per month, an 88% reduction in error rate from the previous average of 113 errors. In addition, the FDA reporting cycle time from start to end went from 25 hours each month to five minutes, a 99.8% reduction in cycle time. Marcus ended up fully automating the FDA reporting process end to end.

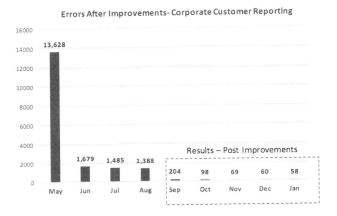

Errors After Improvements- Corporate Customer Reporting

The team ended up winning the Bronze Award for Process Improvement, won the first-place Well-Managed Process Award, was spotlighted across the LICC company intranet system, won the Silver Award for Best Visual Tracking Display, and finally, everyone on the team won LICC's highest award possible, called the Ring of Excellence. During the process, David, the manager of RSRT, was awarded a Business Process Management certification for fully documenting the process.

Recap

For a team that was initially joked about due to such poor quality, RSRT performed such a turnaround in the span of seven months that they achieved nearly perfect numbers. They completely automated an entire process using valuable technical skills that were self-learned and even got positive feedback from a government employee who rarely gave compliments.

To do what was done here took the basic process improvement principles, persistence, and self-confidence.

This turnaround story is as much about the improvement in the personnel as it is about the process error numbers. The lesson learned here is that everyone has the ability in them to improve processes. What it takes is providing the right skills, tools, support, and guidance.

I am proud to state that I was able to look leadership in the eye and tell them confidently that the simple process improvement methodology I regularly preached had worked again, and that the RSRT processes would be sustainable with or without the current team members, a key component of a strong process. Not long after this transformation, David was able to use his newly developed ownership skills to land a leadership position in business development. Marcus, the person without a college degree, became such a valuable and knowledgeable person that he worked his way up to leading an operation with the unique ability to develop his own reports. Management had enough confidence in Miller that he ended up moving into a leadership position, running a larger version of the RSRT team.

CHAPTER 8
STEP 4: *DISCIPLINED EXECUTION*

By this point, most of the hard thinking, exploration, and convincing of people has been completed. Think about it like a Broadway show where the actors have been recruited, the script has been written, the marketing has been distributed, the audience is sitting in their seats, and the stage is set; now, it is time for you to follow the script and deliver.

In my opinion, the hardest of the five steps was Step 2, when you meticulously put together the plan. Now is the time to use that plan you put so much hard work into and make things happen. You have already made people in operations excited and given them hope that you could make their lives better in one way or another. You have convinced leadership that you are the person for this job, and they are even putting resources into supporting the vision that you painted. You have a team of people who are waiting for you to be the catalyst and direct them to make things happen. Now is the time for you to execute. The most important characteristic you will need to demonstrate in Step 4: Disciplined Execution is grit.

[Expect for things not to go as planned, expect there to be complications, and expect there to be late nights to meet your own established aggressive deadlines.]

I have here a list of four common mistakes I have personally made and observed others make during his step—these are things *not* to do.

Common Mistake #1: Getting Distracted

You are walking in the hall and have a 10-minute conversation with someone who gives you a great idea. Either you're convinced that this is a breakthrough idea, or the person you spoke with is a senior person, so you are now feeling the political pressure to incorporate the idea into your project. In a lot of cases, that idea may actually be a decent idea or change of plans, but I would categorize it as a distraction.

Remember, you have already put hours, weeks, and potentially months into getting to this point. You and your teammates have thought through various scenarios, gathered data, and proven the issues you are solving are the most important to focus on. In addition, you have worked the right people to come up with the best solutions. The plan you have already pitched has been approached in the form it is in, and people are counting on you to deliver it.

Trust your methodology and the effort you have already put into this up to this point. Don't get off track, but be disciplined. It is a slippery slope to incorporate new ideas, new concepts, new solutions, new issues, and new things in general at this point.

[As tempting as it may be at the moment, my suggestion is to take the new idea and respectfully push back.]

You can state that you already have an approved plan that you have already begun implementing, but that idea can be incorporated into the next round of changes after you successfully implement what you've already committed to. Remember that this is your project; you own what you deliver and are accountable for it. In addition, if you change at this point, you could begin to lose the confidence of your team, who have been helping you all along up to this point. They will begin to think you can't focus and will easily disregard the inputs they have already provided to you. Simply don't do it. Trust your original plan, and execute with discipline.

Common Mistake #2: Letting Complications Beat You Down

You wake up one day and get a text message that the operational system is down, so all your tech resources will be focused on that for now. Two hours later, your top employee puts in her two-week notice and tells you she took a job offer from a competitor. Then, at the end of the day, you get a call that one of your children is misbehaving at school.

I put that last one in there just to mix in the personal with the professional issues you face because that will happen, and the two will naturally bleed into each other's time. As I stated before, there *will* be issues; they are a normal part of a project and a normal part of life. I suggest you enter your project with the mindset of *expecting* there to be issues, so when they do occur, you understand that it is simply part of the execution process. Mentally prepare for issues to occur, and when they do, be the strong, calm leader for your team's and the project's benefit. Then, from the process improvement project management perspective, when you do come across issues, this is when you need to turn on your problem-solving skills, dig deep, and make things happen.

[Unfortunately, there is no silver bullet to get you through resolving the issues, with the exception of being mentally prepared for them to happen.]

Most of the time, these issues will be the cause of those late nights I warned you about before. Be sure to prepare your family, spouse, and friends for the execution of your project, telling them that urgent things may occur that require your immediate attention. However, I will add that I am a big proponent of the concept that if you plan adequately, nothing should be urgent. The only things that should fall under the 'urgent' status are things that are truly unexpected. Continuously working in urgent or fire-fighting mode is not healthy and a sign of poor leadership and management.

Common Mistake #3: Exploring New Things
You just spent the past few weeks to months exploring lots of new things, and you probably learned how to be pretty good at it. However, a major mistake at this point is to return to this activity. During Step 4: Disciplined Execution, your objective is only to execute the plan that

you have put together.

This is not the time to explore a new idea or even try to learn new things about your business.

[Your objective for this phase, similarly to the other phases, is to be laser-focused on this phase's objective.]

You've already moved beyond the learning about your business phase—that was Step 1: Fact Aggregation. Put it this way: If you begin exploring new things, you are essentially going backwards to Step 1, and if you're doing that, you will need to update your plan and do the pitch again. I know there is no interest in doing that.

This is a great teaching opportunity: In general, don't ever try to multitask. It is best to focus on one thing at a time and be laser-focused until completion. The primary premise of Gary Keller's book *The One Thing*, which talks about his great success from focusing on only one thing at a time, is that "you are successful not due to all the things you do but in the few things you do well."

If you did Step 1 thoroughly, there's no need to explore new areas or re-explore old ones. Stay disciplined with your plan, and again, execute with discipline. As in Common Mistake #1 above, you will be thrown off track, and you may lose your team's confidence.

Common Mistake #4: Waiting until the End to Celebrate

Your project is set to be completed five months from now, but the team has delivered two of the four major efforts. Still, you tell the team you cannot celebrate until you start seeing results or complete the delivery. This is a big mistake for several reasons.

One reason is that, as your process improvement project moves along, people begin to get worn down physically and mentally. A way to replenish this depleted source of energy is to celebrate small wins along the way. This ensures your team feels appreciated.

[This appreciation goes a long way, and if done adequately, respectfully, and genuinely, it can turn into loyalty, trust, and commitment to you.]

People buy into the leader before they buy into the vision.

Another reason you want to celebrate is to use that moment to put everyone back on track and restate the end goal and vision of the project. Look at it like driving your car: You need to continually adjust the steering wheel. You could be charging hard forward, but if in the wrong direction, you will not reach your destination.

The final reason to celebrate is that it continues to create believers in your methodology, in you, and in the vision of the process improvement project. What this will translate into is ownership by team members. This ownership leads to your team caring about the end result, and this care even transfers to after the project ends: Because the team have skin in the game and care, they will be sure to continue watching over the project, doing their part and more. This will significantly increase the chances of your effort's being successful. You are leading this effort, but you are nowhere near doing this alone.

Step 4.1: Begin Execution

No one knows your process improvement effort better than you do—you have put in long hours and mental and physical stress, and you've put yourself out there for people to believe in, but you have yet to deliver anything.

[I would like to commend your efforts up to this point, but I want to help bring us back to reality. It is very easy to convince yourself that you have accomplished something at this point. However, from the perspective of the business, there are no results yet.]

Because I do not know the specific details of your effort, I cannot provide you with a simple way to execute your details, but I can provide you with six tips to maximize your chances of success.

Execution Tip #1: Deliver the Highest Impact First

Your process improvement project is composed of several mini-projects with varying impact levels. When looking at the various impacts you can make and the sub-projects associated with them, prioritize your projects based on the degree of impact to the business. Put the highest-impact items first; don't prioritize based on the easiest or even the order that is sequentially aligned with something.

[This is not a quick-wins-first but a big-wins-first scenario.]

The reason you want to do this is that you must have the perspective that the success of your project is always at risk. The risks are likely out of your control, such as unplanned organizational urgent matters, a change in business priorities, a loss of funding, or a change of heart from leadership. Because of these threats, you should put the most impactful items in the beginning as a form of hedging against the risk of your project being ended prematurely at the 50% mark. In the event your project is pulled out of your control for whatever reason, you and the business can walk away from the project having implemented something tangible, meaningful, and impactful that everyone is proud of.

In addition, with the most impactful items first, if you have already delivered something impactful, your project carries an additional level of credibility, allowing you to make a valid argument not to stop the project.

Multiple times, I have seen a process improvement effort concluded prematurely due to business structure changes or a change in objectives. However, the team and I still ended up delivering some powerful sub-projects that yielded great results that we were all proud of and that the business greatly benefited from.

Execution Tip #2: For Technical or System Changes, Involve Product Managers as Much as Possible

This is probably the most specific piece of advice, but because most process improvement projects incorporate some level of system or technical changes, I would like to share a personal lesson learned.

When delivering your process improvement effort, it is very simple to be convinced that because you and your team know the business, the process, and the project itself best, you are in the best position to drive the system changes. I have made this mistake more than once, but I learned from it and shifted midway through to improve the quality of our deliverables.

What you need to understand is that product managers, or those who are your technical representatives, have objectives that are 100% aligned with yours. Their objective is to make the process as efficient, effective, error-free, and cheap as possible. The more you partner with them, the better and faster you will be able to deliver the items from your process improvement plan. Don't just keep them informed or tell them what you need them to do, but see them as part of the team and required partners to succeed. The earlier you include them, the better your project will be.

Execution Tip #3: Take No Shortcuts
I call this out because I have observed this more than once and have myself fallen into the shortcut trap. As you are executing your plan, you may see that if you skip the fourth of your six steps for a specific project, you will be able to finish faster. This has backfired on me more than once. Trust your judgement from a few weeks earlier when you created your plan.

[You put a lot of thought into it at that stage in a stress-free environment, and now under stress you may not be thinking as clearly, so don't veer off your plan, no matter how tempting it may seem.]

While you were in your stress-free thinking environment, you likely thought through certain risks that are not obvious during your execution mode. The lesson here is, again, stick with your original plan and execute with discipline.

Execution Tip #4: Do Regular Pulse Checks with Your Leaders and with Your Team

I will go into much further detail and elaborate more on this in Step 5. The critical element to think about here is that this is not like a mouse trap, where you set it up, walk away, and then wait for it to catch the mouse. You need to constantly check in with leadership and with your team. You are in a position of leadership and are the one who is ultimately accountable for the success or failure of your project.

The pulse checks you should be executing regularly go both ways. You are providing updates, and simultaneously, you are getting feedback or being fed new information that may or may not be pertinent to your project's success. It is up to you to ascertain what is important and actionable versus just noise.

In addition, these regular pulse checks will ensure that everyone stays bought in throughout the execution phase. It is very easy for you and your efforts to get lost while everyone is waiting for the results. The reason not to get lost is not for reasons of glory, but rather, while leaders and executives are having discussions on prioritization, you don't want your effort to somehow get lost or forgotten in the shuffle, which could lead it to be de-prioritized. Even though the de-prioritization could be unintentional, such decisions are often irreversible. Don't let your process improvement project be forgotten; the simple solution is to perform regular pulse checks.

Execution Tip #5: Push Harder in the Earlier Stages instead of Waiting until Later

I would like you not only to put your highest-impact items in the early stages, but to give your strongest efforts in those stages as well. This is done as a form of risk-mitigation. I regularly see that, in the last two weeks before the deadline or the delivery of a project, everyone is on the edge because meeting the deadline is at risk.

[Instead of making that aggressive push under high mental stress, make that aggressive push when you are not under mental stress.]

You will sense a clear difference in the manner in which you execute, think clearly, and problem solve. You decrease your chances of making mistakes and of missing the deliverable deadlines far down the road, because at this point you have an opportunity to make changes.

Execution Tip #6: Turn on Your Project Risk and Deadline Threat Radar

You will observe that this is a recurring theme. One of your primary roles during Step 4: Discipline Execution is to become a walking radar constantly scanning for things that put your project at risk. Sometimes those risks come from people, funding, leadership, system, industry, or other process changes.

[Risk detection is not difficult to do, but it does not happen by itself. You must do this with true intention.]

If you enter your project with the mindset that you will be constantly scanning for risks, you will do so, and you will catch those risks in advance. There are various ways to do this; I recommend a good combination of setting up triggers and early warning indicators, constantly talking to people up- and downstream of your process, constantly talking to superiors and partners, and building trust with everyone so they share valuable information with you voluntarily. A good leader should have a solid combination of risk indicators coming from systems, people, processes, and data. The important point to take away here is that your risk radar must be intentional.

Step 4.2: Understand What It Takes to Execute

Some people believe that there are certain people who are flat-out effortlessly better than everyone else; they are often referred to as *naturals*. However, there is no one out there that reaches the highest level of his or her craft without putting in crazy hours and, in particular, grit. Grit is what it will take for you to have a successful execution. Don't believe that the execution will be easy because you have lots of experience and know your industry or your field. From my experience, each and every process improvement project has its own character and almost a sub-culture associated with it. You are constantly learning, and in some cases, wisdom from previous projects can translate to your new project. But there is a strange way that a reset button is pushed for each individual process improvement effort, so your credibility, support, resources, effectiveness, efficiency, and trustworthiness have to be regained each time separately and sometimes via different methods. My main point is that you will need to respect the process improvement project and all its components to the degree that you *never take your eye off the ball*. Work with a degree of intensity, respect and grit to ensure the success of the entire project. If you do this, not only will your project be successful, but you will continue to be given the opportunity to work on future projects, career growth, and the reputation you deserve.

Sometimes we are somehow convinced that certain people are flat-out more talented than others, but it is likely their level of effort that lead to their success rather than their talent. Super stars who achieve over and over generally put in super effort. In her book *Grit*, Angela Duckworth proves scientifically with a plethora of evidence that the most accomplished and successful people are *grittier* than everyone else. There is a great formula in her book that I would like to share to show the relationship between talent and achievement:

$$[Talent \times Effort = Skill$$
$$Skill \times Effort = Achievement]$$

Talent is only one factor, and without effort, it doesn't translate into skill. Even if you are not naturally very talented, you can still develop skill with effort. However, skill alone does not lead to achievement—you need still more effort.

My final point regarding Step 4 is to execute with a gritty mentality and have a disciplined execution. The next case study is a great example of a process improvement effort that took a high degree of discipline and grit.

CHAPTER 9
CASE STUDY 5: *PROCESS SEQUENCE RESTRUCTURING FOR INCREASED CAPACITY AND IMPROVED CUSTOMER EXPERIENCE*

This case takes place with Shining Star Securities Management Firm, where I served as head of the Asset Recoveries Operations Department. Shining Star Securities Management Firm (SSSMF) was a purchaser of debt from large banks for pennies to the dollar, and the portfolio I managed consisted of loans to Information Technology (IT) companies that had defaulted on their payments for their high-value server infrastructure. The loans I managed were in default, and my team's focus was to work out arrangements with the original IT companies to let other IT companies purchase their equipment for a lower price from us if we were able to work out a deal. The alternative was letting the original IT company go into complete default on the loan, leading us to need to liquidate the securities, and we would end up repossessing the equipment and selling it ourselves.

The Asset Recoveries Operations Department (AROD) had existed for a few years now at SSSMF, but getting into high-value server infrastructure loans was a new venture for us, so there were immature processes in place and only satisfactory knowledge of the industry. Katerina, the manager of the operations who reported directly to me, was an industry veteran we had recruited from a competitor. Her industry experience combined with my operational management and process improvement experience seemed like a good match to help us turn this operation into something bullet-proof we were all proud of.

The need for a major transformation was initially driven by the fact that senior management would ask for the number of loans that were liquidated, how many arrangements closed each month, and a forecast for future months. These numbers had a high importance because they would help the finance department with loss forecasting and loss reporting to the Treasury Department. Wildly incorrect numbers could lead to the government accusing us of hiding losses, and that was a path we wanted to avoid.

Background Information

As with most process improvement efforts, there were several layers to the onion that needed to be revealed and resolved before fixing the downstream impacts. As I began digging into the data, I realized that, in order get an idea of our number of liquidations and arrangements, we needed to know how many files we even had, and who those files were assigned to on the AROD team. The personnel who worked out arrangements with customers were called arrangement consultants (ACs), and they received incentives for each arrangement they completed. It surprised me that even this information was difficult to get a handle on. Then, as I began to ask questions about what the process steps were from start to end, I received different answers from the various ACs. In addition, aside from the process issues, there appeared to be a declining number of arrangements being completed, which indicated higher losses for SSSMF.

To summarize, the problems I gathered that I was responsible for resolving included the following:

1) Improve forecasting accuracy of liquidations and arrangements.
2) Improve pipeline management capabilities to increase efficiency and give more loans to better performers.
3) Increase the capacity of the team.

The initial data revealed the following:

- There were 514 active loans indicated in the system per initial reporting. However, we knew that our ACs were not working 514 loans. Nonetheless, in the initial phases, we did not have a good grasp on which loans were in which status.

- There were 274 loans in default across the company that were assigned to non-AC personnel. This meant that either they were not being worked but should have been or they were categorized incorrectly.

- We had 213 loans with a processing age of 200 or more days old. This indicated an inefficient and ineffective process.

- There were 204 loans that needed funds to be cleared to the correct status after the closing of an arrangement. Those 204 loans represented $464,000 in funds that were sitting in an incorrect status, waiting to be correctly applied.

- There were on average 70 referrals coming from the upstream process, which led to an average of 33 arrangement closings per month. A referral indicated that the original IT Company showed interest in making an arrangement.
- In addition, for referrals that did not turn into arrangements and ended up getting denied or liquidated, we had no insight into why. This lack of visibility was frustrating when trying to increase throughput.
- The cycle time of the process from end to end was around 75 days.

The initial data revealed we had a lot of opportunities to improve, and the gamut of areas to improve upon spanned widely. I began where I always start when I encounter scenarios like this: I developed an agreed-upon process flow map of the current state process.

The Approach
After I developed the process flow of the current state, I went to Office Depot and printed out an extremely large copy of the detailed current state process flow and attached it to the wall. I held an all-day meeting with Katerina and one of the more senior ACs. What we ended up doing for half of that day with that giant process flow diagram was draw all over it. We identified process gaps, duplications in the process, a lack of process controls, and potential areas of opportunity to dig deeper into. We ended up developing a 'future state' process flow diagram of what we wanted the process to look like in the future. Then we developed a list of items that had to happen in order for us to turn that future state process flow diagram into reality.

I then educated the team on pipeline management and identified that some ACs were more skilled than others, but we were not utilizing the more skilled ACs to their potential, given how we were assigning loans. Finally, given that we did not have any funds or even the time to develop a snazzy pipeline management reporting infrastructure, what I did was personally commit to developing it myself using spreadsheets from the ground up. However, in order to develop the pipeline management tool effectively, we first had to ensure that our numbers in the system were accurate, and in addition, I proposed we incorporate stage tracking in the system. This stage tracking meant that we would be able to quickly tell what stage the processing of the arrangement was in, as in 1) un-referred, 2) referred, 3) being decided, 4) approved, 5) scheduled to close, and 6) closed.

The plan of attack to improve our various opportunities boiled down to the five following areas to improve:
1) Increase the capacity and efficiency of ACs.
2) Reduce digital and physical clutter.
3) Resolve inaccurate information in the system and improve reporting.
4) Eliminate rework, wasted production time, and overproduction.
5) Improve communications without adding time commitments within the AROD team, management, or senior management.

These five major buckets overlapped in some cases and in other cases required independent solutions. Instead of assigning ownership of specific projects to different people, Katerina and I decided to work together on each effort to maximize our synergies based on our knowledge and skills. This transformational effort ended up taking approximately a year to deliver the results, but once realized, all parties were satisfied.

The Execution

When Katerina and I approached the five aspects of the process we would be putting our energy towards, we knew it would be a challenging effort. The process had been relatively mature, and improvements are generally harder to obtain for mature processes because there isn't much low-hanging fruit.

[We realized that the initial three problems we set out to resolve improved forecasting accuracy and pipeline management and increased capacity, but had issues deeply embedded under several layers of other problems.]

We would be required to shock the system, and that would include moving things around and challenging everyone to be open-minded to operating in a different way. This shock-the-system mentality led us to experiment as well.

Addressing Capacity

To address the capacity issue, we used a technique generally used in the manufacturing world for the handling of material flow through the process. We implemented something called a 'pull' system, as opposed to the 'push' system that was in place at the time. A push system is the method of assigning loans to employees evenly based on the total pipeline available, whereas new loans enter the pipeline, they continue to be distributed evenly in a round-robin manner. As the name suggests, available work is essentially pushed out to the employees.

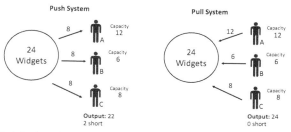

Push versus Pull Systems for Work Assignment

Round robin technique used and everyone assigned work evenly

Employees 'pull' work as they complete, maximizing employee potential

On the contrary, a pull system, requires employees to pull for new work as it comes in from the available pipeline, but they need to complete their currently assigned work first. One important detail regarding the deployment of the pull system for assigning loans is that ACs would receive the next loan in the pipeline blindly without any way to influence the loan they would work on. This blind-assignment element was critical for keeping the integrity of the system by preventing any favoritism from being shown in the assignment of loans. This was important because some loans, depending their specific details, required more work and time to complete than others. In collaboration with the existing incentive system, ACs were incentivized to work more loans. This was the type of system that top performers preferred and lower performers did not like. The big benefit from such an assignment method is that the overall throughput is increased due to higher performers' being given the liberty to take on more work while lower performers continue to perform at the same pace.

After a few months of implementation, as people got used to the change in working loans, they began to appreciate the method and the system's cleanness.

Addressing Clutter
Now, to address clutter and organization, we implemented

a paper-free environment. Prior to our changes, ACs would work physical files containing all pertinent information, which they would print out and place in a manila folder. This would often lead to stacks of folders and papers on people's desks, and when an AC was out of the office, there were downstream issues that were created. We made it mandatory for ACs to work their files directly from the system, so reading the information and note-taking took place in our record system. Rolling out this new policy took significant effort, from the initial transition with what was currently being worked through new files. We initially received a significant amount of pushback from ACs, as having a physical printout gave them a sense of comfort. We assured them that there would be no change, but now they would be reading the information off their screens. To accompany this change, we purchased additional monitors for everyone on the team so their productivity wouldn't be impacted. Some folks requested three screens, and some were comfortable with two. To complete this change, we developed a one-page document for all ACs to put on their desk that stated "My Office Space is Cleaned and in Compliance." At the end of the day, we required all desks to be cleaned and clear of any paper or clutter, and the ACs would place that clean desk document on their desk to indicate that their cabinet drawers had been locked and their desktop was clear of any clutter. We put a basic rotational program in place, where a different AC was responsible each week for walking around the space and ensuring all desk spaces were compliant. That person responsible for the validation would send a confirmation email to Katerina at the end of each day. Any findings were addressed appropriately by Katerina as the manager of the team.

To accompany this clean-up mentality, Katerina and I took two solid weeks of our time to go through every loan in default assigned to an AC or a non-AC. What we did then was to digitally clean up our pipeline. We realized a large percentage of loans that should have been closed were still open in the system, loans that should have been worked were not assigned appropriately, and loans that were labeled incorrectly were not being worked correctly. There was no magic nor any special skills required for us to do this, just basic due diligence, and we took the time to do something that should have been a normal habit for everyone. We ended up removing, closing out, or reassigning approximately 50% of the files in the system. There was a digital mess much like the physical mess. Consequently, we trained our team on how to be organized and disciplined.

Addressing Reporting

Now, in terms of data, we had no budget, nor any data reporting analysts available to us in a timely manner to help us build out strong reporting. As a result, I personally developed a manual tracking tool for Katerina to use to manage her team's pipeline. The tool was a spreadsheet consisting of several tabs containing the data and one tab making the appropriate calculations and displaying that information in a way that was useful.

Pipeline Output of Reporting Tool

Employee	Assigned	Approved	Not Closing	Closed	Projected	< 30 days	30-59 days	60-89 days	90+ days	Totals	EOM Final Forecast
						Decision Timeline Still Open					
Alice	16	8	8	1	1	7	8	4	2	21	1
Ronnie	12	4	10	3	3	11	6	9	0	26	2
Cliff	13	8	9	3	5	7	14	1	1	23	5
Thomas	8	2	9	3	3	9	4	4	0	17	2
JJ	17	8	6	5	5	7	10	4	0	21	5
Norman	17	14	6	8	10	8	6	1	1	16	7
Sam	19	13	8	5	5	12	5	6	1	24	5
Chuck	13	7	5	11	9	4	10	9	2	25	6
TOTAL	115	64	61	39	41	65	63	38	7	173	33

There was a little bit of complexity in building out the spreadsheet tool; however, the benefit was that Katerina was able to quickly see how many loans were in each status, how many loans would be closing on each date, how many loans were in the pipeline, and how many loans were assigned to each AC. The manual tracking tool was not perfect and had occasional lag but was a huge leap forward from what existed before. In addition, it was accurate and let us see trends and performance, and we had an ability to forecast volumes so we could prepare appropriately. Another benefit was that the data gave us an opportunity to conduct further analysis on reasons for declines, reasons for delays, common errors, etc., and with this powerful information, we were able to make informed decisions.

The manual tracking tool eventually turned into our performance dashboard, which senior management wanted to see on a daily basis.

[We had up-to-date statistics on average cycle times between each status, overall cycle times, and error rates and were able to objectively compare AC performance. The purpose of the manual tracking tool to serve our need at that time, given the resource constraints presented to us.]

A few years later, the manual tracking tool was replaced with a more advanced and refined version using SQL and special software, but it was essentially the same tool, though it wasn't in a spreadsheet format and didn't require manual data entry.

Addressing Rework
To address rework took some roll-up-your-sleeves process work. We used what we had mapped previously and then extended that mapping to the processes prior to the loan's getting to the ACs. We then used that information to categorize the primary tasks of the upfront processes and, in the same format, the primary tasks of ACs.

We observed something that was not very evident, but when we caught it, we were able to remove steps from prior processes and move them over to ACs: Prior to a loan's being referred to ACs, there were three sets of documents ordered from vendors, and it was not until those three documents were received that they were allowed to be officially passed on to ACs. However, those three sets of documents were often problematic or incorrect and required the AC to go back to the vendor that had provided the documents to correct them. This back and forth added about 10 days of cycle time to the overall process in the form of rework. In addition to the added cycle time, the prior process was limited in what could be referred to ACs because of the requirement to order and receive these documents.

We made the bold move of working with prior processes and making a change in the process: We would transfer the responsibility for ordering those three documents from them to us. Initially, ACs were not very happy about this, but it didn't take long for them to realize that it made their lives easier because there was no longer any back and forth with the vendors that provided the documents because they were right the first time. The ACs knew exactly what they needed and asked them for the exact items in the exact format they needed for their purpose. The vendors were happy as well. This process shift led to a reduction in cycle time of 10 days, and a bonus was that this also led to an increase in the pipeline of referrals because what was required for a file to be considered referred had lessened.

Shifting of Task Work to Speed Up Cycle Time

| Tasks Employee 1 | Tasks Employee 2 |

Before Changes

- Send package
- Receive offer
- Request docs
- Gather docs
- Forward docs

- Work with agent
- Work with insurance
- Negotiate
- Close

After Changes

- Send package
- Receive offer

- Work with agent
- Work with insurance
- Negotiate
- Close

- Request docs
- Gather docs
- Forward docs

Addressing Communication

We observed that communication from management to employees, employees to management, management to senior management, and even from employee to employee was often lacking, incorrect, and late. We came up with some original yet simple and cheap solutions. We implemented visual aids that were maintained by the ACs but benefited managers, senior managers, and ACs alike.

There was a series of visual tools that we developed and trained the ACs to maintain:

1) A forecasting and visual indicator of closings: This essentially was a calendar where ACs would indicate with a unique magnetic sticker a scheduled closing and then, with a different unique magnetic sticker, an actual closing. We could see that certain days were crowded with stickers, and we could also quickly see who had put them there.

2) A loan assignment board: This showed exactly

how many loans each AC had and how many were in each status. Those statuses included how many were assigned, how many active, how many submitted for approval, how many approved, how many projected to close, and how many actually closed.

3) Goals board: At the beginning of each week, Katerina would indicate a goal for the team and then how many were actually produced against those goals, as well as what our cycle times were. She would use the information from the loan assignment board to populate this. This board gave me, as the head of the department, a very easy way to see how we were tracking without ever having to ask anyone.

We would meet together as a team on a daily basis and talk through the metrics on our boards. We rotated who was responsible for leading the daily meeting as a form of ensuring that everyone knew the information and of giving each person an opportunity to serve in some leadership capacity.

An additional form of communication improvement was that we had the documented process visually posted on every AC's desk.

[Even though most were very experienced, the process was still complex, so to help them be self-sufficient, we wanted them to be able to answer their own questions about what step was next in certain scenarios.]

The process flow diagrams on their desks would also be

updated as we made process changes, and they served as a reference point for us to discuss in our daily meeting when there was a disagreement or change. I would sometimes observe ACs taking a copy of the process flow diagram to show one of their peers why what the other was doing was wrong. It was a beautiful image to see them talk about their processes, and I could see they felt a sense of ownership of their own results and process. This is analogous to the new form of industrial building design that exposes all the piping and metal works in the ceilings to give you an idea of what is holding the building together, or similarly, those elevators with glass walls so that you can see all the gears working.

Finally, a small nuance that was informative, fun, and potentially annoying to some other departments was that any time there an arrangement was officially closed, that AC would ring a cowbell. This made the whole team excited for the opportunity to show their peers that they had closed something. From a management perspective, I was able to tell when things were very busy and slow simply based on cowbell sounds.

We had various forms of improvement in ways to communicate with each other and with people outside the department about how things were going via boards, charts, process flows, and bells without an incredible amount of effort. However, these simple methods created a sense of transparency and awareness for everyone on the AROD team. We were in a state where everyone on the team knew exactly how many closings we had, who had the most, and how much faster we were last week than this. In addition, management and even a random person passing by would be privy to that same information without asking anyone, simply by observing the boards.

The Results

All these efforts took months to implement, and we had the benefit of experiencing people's growth and seeing the process gradually improve over time. I am a process person at heart, and I get most of my satisfaction in the creation process rather than from the results in the end. I also get great satisfaction from seeing people's growth as they achieve more than they could before. In the end, we built something that we were all very proud of and that generated some of the most remarkable results.

Aside from the apparent visual organizational improvements and the increase in positive energy in the group, we had some great numbers at the end of this story:

1) We reduced 100% of all miscategorized active loans and reduced them from the 514 shown in the system to the 184 that represented what was truly active. This was a 64% reduction.

2) We had a 93% reduction in loans assigned to non-ACs. Before, we had 274 loans assigned to non-ACs, and we ended with 19. Those final 19 took more time to unravel, and we were unable to systemically retract them from the non-ACs.

3) We reduced the number of loans aged more than 200 days by 85%. We previously had 213, and we ended up with 31.

4) We cleared the funds sitting in a particular queue requiring extensive work that had been there for years from $464,000 down to $33,000. This was a 93% reduction and was money that went back into the business.

5) We had a 24% increase in the number of closings per month, which were derived from an increase in arrangement referrals. Where before we averaged 33 arrangements closed per month, we ended up consistently averaging 41 per month.

The impressive part about this is that ACs have no influence on the volume—we essentially created more closings with the same volume upstream. We performed data analysis on what was preventing arrangements from closing and made changes in the process accordingly.

6) We reduced our cycle time by over 10 days, which represented a 23% decrease in cycle time from 75 to 58 days.

There were other improvements that are difficult to quantify, such as improvements in organization, cleanliness, our ability to communicate the status of the process quickly and clearly to senior management, and our ability to quickly understand where we stood as a department at any moment. Essentially, the department became much easier to manage, and ACs on the team got to focus on being ACs rather than on various administrative tasks.

Recap
An effort of this magnitude and over this span of time is taxing, but in the end, the ACs, the manager (Katerina), and I established a set of operations that were sustainable for years to come. When we began this transformation, the initial concern was that senior management didn't understand what the status of the process was and couldn't forecast financial figures.

[As with most successful process improvements, if we had just focused on quickly addressing senior management's concerns, we would have been guaranteed to have other problems later.]

It took the peeling-one-layer-at-a-time approach to really get to the cores of the issues and address each of them head on. We used some tools along the way, but nothing complicated that average people couldn't understand or execute. With the right mindset, any process or operation can be transformed.

CHAPTER 10
STEP 5: *CONTINUOUS COMMUNICATION*

You are almost at the finish line. You are not done yet, but you can hear the roar of people cheering as they wait for you to break that ribbon. The hardest work has already taken place, but that does not make this step any less important or less critical to the success of the project. This is the fifth and final step of the *Simplified Process Improvement* approach. One detail I will add is that this step actually begins approximately 30–50% into Step 4 while you are executing but continues on even beyond execution completion.

I hear it in meetings and especially in off-the-record side conversations that we don't communicate enough, and when we do communicate, we don't include all the right people. They are essentially saying that a culture of transparency is preferred and likely more effective for a well-run business and project. You may have heard a few times that you can never over-communicate. However, the approach that I recommend is a version of over-communicating, and if you begin to have people tell you that you are communicating too much, in my opinion, that is a good sign. At least no one will be able to make the criticism that they were not kept in the loop.

[To be on the safe side, I would suggest you lean towards higher frequency of communication and a larger audience size.]

There is a slight increase in work with higher frequency, but expanding your audience size creates no increase in workload. And if you use a standard template and always communicate the same elements, as I will cover next, the amount of work to create your communications should be minimal. On the other hand, though, I suggest you make sure that you produce high-quality content.

[Just keep in mind that most of the people you are communicating with are not involved in your day-to-day operations, so communication becomes representative of your project. Take pride in your work.]

Some of the elements of communication were covered in Step 2, when you put thought into communication as you put together your process improvement plan. We will cover some of the specifics of the communication plan, but continuous communication is move expansive than the communication plan alone. I will begin by covering a) the separate audiences communicated with and b) the frequency of those communications.

Your Audiences
There are three separate audiences that your communications should be tailored for. What I mean by "be tailored for" is that you should be communicating different types of information depending on the audience's roles and objectives.

Audience #1: Your Team: This is the group of people that are directly under your leadership and are primary members and contributors to the process improvement project. They may not be reporting directly to you but are dedicated to the project and thus are part of the team. Your communications with your team should be as detailed as possible, and your role for them is to eliminate any road blocks or issues that may prevent them from executing. When there is an issue, they should be the first group of people to know.

Audience #2: Peers and Partners: These are the people that are part of support groups, who don't necessarily support the project but report to the same manager as you and thus have some skin in the game. The communications with this group of people should be less detailed than those with your team, but be sure to provide them with information relevant to the general progress of the project. This group will represent a great opportunity to test and refine your influence skills because you will be relying heavily on them. However, they are not under your leadership. Given this fact, many of your interactions with them should be with a grateful and respectful approach. Don't just communicate with your partners but with their managers as well—their managers need to know that they are involved in your project and that their contributions are important to the success of your project, which is important to the business.

Audience #3: Superiors, Leaders, and Sponsors: This is the group of people that are not necessarily part of your daily operations but do have a lot of skin in the game, given that they have offered their resources to you to deliver something. Because they are not involved in day-to-day operations means you shouldn't overwhelm them with those details. Focus on high-level points and consistently provide the same information.

Frequency

You should be very cognizant regarding the frequency of communications. As mentioned earlier, I would rather you over-communicate than under-communicate. A high degree of transparency is a good practice in general. However, depending on the audience you are communicating with, I suggestion varying the frequency, because the communications serve different purposes.

You should have a high frequency of communication with Audience #1, your team. It does not need to be as formal, and most of the time written communication is not necessary. The level of communication with your team will mostly come in the form of short **daily meetings**. Finally, when you communicate with Audience #2, you should also include Audience #1, but not necessarily when you communicate with Audience #3.

I suggest a weekly communication frequency with peers and partners. If it is possible to get a recurring weekly in-person meeting with these people, that would be ideal. If you struggle with this, what I suggest is that you hold **bi-weekly in-person meetings** but still continue with weekly written communications. The details and contents of those written communications are covered in the subsequent pages.

The least frequent form of communications should be reserved for superiors, leaders, and sponsors. This is not because your project is not important to them, but rather because you want to provide meaningful and meaty updates with great content and progress to share. With higher communication frequencies, there is less progress but more tactical things to share. If possible, make your best effort to establish a monthly in-person check-in, if not with all the applicable leaders, then at least with a few who have the most to gain from your process improvement project. In addition to the in-person meetings, I suggest you also provide all members of Audience #3 with your written monthly updates.

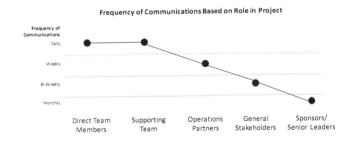

There are different strategies, approaches, and expectations for the different groups of people because they each serve different roles for the success of the project.

[In addition, those different parties have something they want to take away from your process improvement project's efforts, so if it doesn't meet their needs, your communication may be overlooked.]

As I mentioned earlier, you want to begin communicating approximately 30–50% into the execution phase. I will cover which types of communication I recommend throughout as execution progresses through post-delivery.

Step 5.1: Establish Communication Rapport
Step 5.1 occurs when you are 30–50% into execution. Your objective during this phase as it pertains to continuous communication is to set up your communication channels and to establish a rapport with all stakeholders. I will add, when I mention the word *communications*, I am referring to documents, emails, formal meetings, and informal meetings or discussions.

The following should serve as a baseline for your communications during Step 5.1.

Branded One-Page Update
Purpose/Content: This will be a document that you and others will be able to reference down the road as evidence of the work you've put in and as a way to clearly see progress. The reason I call it 'branded' is that you should give the document a particular look, so if you have a team name, put it in the document. Ensure the document has a clean yet informative look. The basic content that should be included in your one-page update is as follows:

a) High-level project status in the form of words.

b) Sub-project status, in the form of colors.

c) Items that have been fully implemented.

d) Something interesting, educational, and clever to share regarding the learnings or discoveries from the work.

e) Any risks that you may have identified.

f) Recognition of key players between the latest update and the one being sent.

g) What you plan on completing by the next update.

Delivery Method: This should be a clean document, preferably in the form of an un-editable PDF so it maintains its form and structure as others view it or print it out.

Frequency: I recommend that this update be distributed on a bi-weekly to monthly basis. This branded one-page update will continue to be sent from this point through the end of execution completion of the project. However, whatever frequency you land on, be sure to be consistent with that frequency because people will begin to expect it.

Audience: Your audience for this document should be every stakeholder, from the team members to partners (and their managers) to the leaders. If your updates are of high quality and you have something meaningful to share, you will observe that people even begin to reference your update document and, as an added bonus, even use it in some cases to show how well the project is going.

Daily Team Meetings
Purpose/Content: You want to hold a meeting with your team on a daily basis. Its purpose is to educate you about any roadblocks they may be facing and to allow you to communicate anything new you may be aware of. You should also use this time to inspire and motivate your team. You as the leader are key to ensuring that their energy levels and efforts continue.

Delivery Method: This should come in the form of a physical meeting. It can take place in a room that you have reserved for your project, or you can stand up in same place each time.

Frequency: This should take place daily and should be quick, no longer than 15 minutes. It should be something your team looks forward to but should not be the only manner in which your team can get ahold of you.

Audience: The meeting should consist of your team each day, but inform your team that they are open to bring guests when there are certain topics for those guests to cover. You will find that the business begins to catch on to your daily meetings and uses them as the time to get ahold of you and your team together; this is OK.

Weekly Partners Meetings
Purpose/Content: The purpose of this weekly meeting with your partners is less about updates and more to serve as a working session. You will use this meeting to give your team access to partners and give partners access to your team. Keep in mind that your partners could consist of technology, attorneys, compliance, risk partners, production operations, marketing, and others that provide some form of support to the project.

Delivery Method: This should come in the form of a physical meeting or a phone call, as necessary. Reserve a common room or place for everyone to meet so that it becomes a tradition.

Frequency: This should take place on a weekly basis, and reserve an hour. You may not need to take the whole hour each time, but there may some deep working sessions that use all that time.

Audience: The meeting should always consist of your team as well as all your partners. Make it clear that they are not all required to attend, but that this window of time will have a somewhat open-door policy, so anyone can come as needed.

Monthly Leaders Meetings

Purpose/Content: The primary purpose of this meeting is a one-way communication from you to the leaders to provide an update. During this meeting, your objective is to communicate the status of the project, make clear any risks, and if you have any additional requests, this is when you can make them. What you cover should be consistent with your branded one-page update.

Delivery Method: This should come in the form of a physical meeting, but depending on your leadership's physical location, that may not be possible. A phone call or teleconference may be required.

Frequency: This should take place monthly. If you find it extremely difficult to meet with your leadership, I don't recommend you meet less frequently than every six weeks.

Audience: For most cases, you will be the only representative from your team, but there may be special circumstances when you want your team or certain team members to attend. This could be when there is a certain topic you would like one of your team members to cover or when you would like to recognize someone.

Step 5.2: Begin Communicating Preliminary Results

You should continue with all the elements covered in Step 5.1. Step 5.2 occurs at 75–100% completion of the execution phase.

Preliminary and Early Results

Purpose/Content: Once you reach this phase, you should be sourcing and finding your primary metrics, which were determined in Step 2. In addition, monitor ancillary metrics. You should include highlights in an easy-to-follow format to distribute, but on a separate file that you do not share, also monitor other metrics important to the health of the primary metrics. These typically serve as leading indicators. A benefit of beginning to monitor your results at this stage is that, in the event you have difficulty finding a way to monitor data, you still have to problem-solve that.

Delivery Method: This should be delivered to primary stakeholders and your team in the form of a one-page document, again as a PDF. The document should be branded similarly to your other documents so it looks consistent.

Frequency: I recommend these updates be distributed monthly, but your team should be very in tune with the results. You should be open to giving your team access to the results on a daily basis in a less formal format.

Audience: The audience for this document would be the leaders (Audience #3), along with your team. It would be a separate communication from the one-page update because of this document's very specific purpose.

Step 5.3: Celebrate

At this point, you can conclude your meetings from Step 5.1.

This is moment when you can take a pause and celebrate because the hardest work, and 99% of all the work, is completed. One note, though, is that you are celebrating the completion of the project, not celebrating a turnaround or great results (yet).

There are a couple routes to make your celebration worthwhile. You can do both or only one.

Celebration #1
In this celebration, I recommend you hold a 30-minute to

one-hour meeting with the superiors, leaders, and sponsors, along with your primary team. Make that get-together meaningful for both your team and the leaders. Be sure you recognize your team in front of the leaders, calling out specific things each person did to contribute. The more specific the better. Follow this up by calling out the partners who helped you to deliver (even though they will not be in the room).

Then transition into providing something that the leaders can take away and feel proud of up to this point. Provide a quick verbal overview of the work you and the team did to get to this point and then provide some of your preliminary results to them. They will be happy to hear that you are proactively monitoring without needing someone to ask for it. Conclude your overview and preliminary results with assurance that you will continue to monitor the results, will provide them with monthly updates, and will make it clear to them when you can call the entire project a success. As uninvolved as the leaders have been up to this point, this is their favorite part of the entire project: They are interested in the results their investments are leading to. Be sure to communicate to them what metrics you will include during the monitoring phase.

Celebration #2
This is a celebration that you should do with your team, as well as your partners who have made contributions to the project. There's no need to be stingy with recognition at this point—it is cheap but greatly appreciated. This celebration should be less formal, and you as the leader should provide your sincere gratitude to everyone and throw out some specific problems the team faced and overcame. Everyone will be proud of this and will be able to connect to you and the effort.

Step 5.4: Post-Implementation

Continuous Monitoring

Continue to provide the results to the leaders and your team, as you stated you would in Step 5.3. At this point, it is possible if not likely that you will be pulled into your normal day job or another project, but it is absolutely critical that you do not take your eye off monitoring the results, not only to declare victory, but to ensure that things don't get off track. It is not likely but possible that results could get worse because of a change your project made. If you do observe something going in the wrong direction, I would not jump into panic mode—wait for three solid trending data points to validate this. Noise in the form of data moving up and down is common, but three continuous data points in the wrong direction is a trend.

Achieved Results

When you are in a place to declare victory based on validated data, you can send your final communication with a victory-sounding tone in the form of a written document shared with all three audiences. In the body, be sure to include one or two highlighted metrics that clearly demonstrate your victory and to tie your victory declaration back to the original plan, business case, and benefits you claimed there would be.

Optional Additional Celebration

Depending on the level of results, you may be able to convince leadership to fund a nice celebration for all the critical people involved in the success. Your project may have saved millions of dollars, eliminated a problem the company had been facing for years, made the process faster enough to give you a competitive edge, or driven awesome customer experience results. Whatever the result(s) may be, you should be extremely proud of what you and your team have accomplished.

[Few people get to truly experience a business transformation as a result of their direct efforts. This is a feat you should justly be proud of.]

That wraps up Step 5: Continuous Communication. I will restate five of the most important tips as they relate to this final step.

1. Understand that your communications are a **powerful tool** to navigate the perception everyone has of your project. What you put down will be what is discussed.
2. Be cognizant of who **your audience** is when communicating and understand what they want and what you want them to take away.
3. **Take pride** in the quality of your communications. They may be the only source of information some people have about your project.
4. Please do **over-communicate**, both in frequency and in audience-size.
5. Your project is not considered a success until you have provided **evidence in the form of results**. So don't stop communicating just because the execution has been completed.

You should be very proud of yourself that you've made it this far. You've accomplished quite a lot for your business, and in addition, you've enhanced your own personal and professional credibility. Chances are you got to meet new people you may not have interacted with before (thus expanding your network). As you went into battle with people, you built strong relationships. You definitely learned a lot of new things about your business and had new experiences that will help you continue to grow.

One last comment is that most people don't get the opportunity to lead process improvement projects, and most of the time this is because they believe their title doesn't require or allow it.

[The primary point of this book is to tell you that you can be a process improvement practitioner, no matter your role. Don't let your title or job description limit you.]

One of the most personally fulfilling things you can do in your career is to lead a process improvement project from inception through completion and actually deliver results. An overwhelming majority of people will not experience this in their lives. Go for it!

CHAPTER 11
CLOSING

Did you know that in the second quarter of 2017 there were two billion active Facebook users? Did you know that as of 2017 there are 500 million tweets *per day*? Did you know there are 3.25 billion hours of YouTube video viewed per month? The first point is, those are **big numbers**, and the second point is that the sources of these numbers are **social media**. These are sources that *everyone* has **free access** to. Those people that have free access to them include *your customers*.

With social media connecting the entire world and literally at the fingertips of your customers, one bad experience can be detrimental to your business. All it would take is one YouTube video that goes viral stating how many errors there are when working with your company, or a Facebook post from one of your customers indicating how slow it is working with you and including some specific reasons why that has been shared across thousands to millions of accounts.

However, there is some good that can come from social media as well. Let's say your business delivers some of the best experiences your customers have ever experienced. By coincidence, one of your customers happens to be someone with 10 million followers on his or her Twitter account. This customer decides to tweet that your company not only delivers a high-quality product but delivers it fast and at a decent price. This one tweet from this one customer could be what takes your business to unimaginable levels that you never thought possible.

There is one theme here. High quality, fast production, low costs, and great experiences are all driven by great processes! More often than not, we think we can sell our way to success and then simply let the rest fall into place. Unfortunately, reality doesn't work this way—all successful businesses need to have a stellar front end and a bullet-proof back end.

Whether you are an entrepreneur, a small business owner, a junior player in the business space, or an experienced professional with a specific need, *Simplified Process Improvement: The Art of Process Improvement Decoded into Five Simple Steps* was written for you. It was written to help you translate the complexity typically associated with process improvement practices and to bring to light tips that are often only shared within process improvement communities.

Every organization can benefit from improving its processes, yet very few proactively take action to make it happen. Be the one to drive those improvements.

[Unplanned process improvement is wishful thinking.]

ABOUT THE AUTHOR

Eduardo Perez is an operations and process improvement leader with over 15 years of operational and corporate experience. Eduardo is an expert in leadership and process improvement practices and has won several awards for his business turnaround achievements. Eduardo has saved the companies he has worked for millions of dollars, helping them significantly reduce errors and improve their cycle times, improving the customer experience. He has held various leadership positions across the manufacturing, technology, and financial services industries. He is certified as a Six Sigma Black Belt (CSSBB), Lean Practitioner, Project Management Professional (PMP), and Certified Quality Engineer (CQE). In 2016, Eduardo was awarded the 40 Under 40 **Young Hispanic Corporate Achievers (YHCA) Award.** Eduardo currently runs a YouTube channel and the website/blog, www.theprocessman.com.

Eduardo is the founder and principal consultant of TPM Consulting Group, which helps small businesses and entrepreneurs survive the growth curve by helping them establish a strong operational foundation. For more information visit, http://www.tpmconsultinggroup.com/.

Eduardo resides in Texas with his wife and two children. In his free time, he has served as President of a Dallas-Fort Worth Hispanic organization chapter consisting of 800 members and was also national lead of a Hispanic professional organization consisting of 3,000 members, with responsibility for strategy, a mentorship program, community efforts, the budget, and engagement. Eduardo also serves as an active leader at his local church.

To get a hold of Eduardo for consulting, speaking, training, and other opportunities, visit
www.tpmconsultinggroup.com.

BIBLIOGRAPHY

Covey, Stephen R. *The 7 Habits of Highly Effective People*. Franklin Covey, 1998.

Phillips, Donald T. *Lincoln on Leadership*. Warner Books, 1992.

Collins, Jim. *Good to Great: Why Some Companies Make the Leap... and Others Don't*. Random House, 2001.

Willink, Jocko, and Leif Babin. *Extreme Ownership: How U.S. Navy SEALs Lead and Win*. St. Martin's Press, 2017.

Perez, Eduardo. "5 Ways to Focus in a Distracting World." *LinkedIn*, 10 May 2017, www.linkedin.com/pulse/5-ways-focus-distracting-world-eduardo-perez/

Schafer, Jack, and Marvin Karlins. *The like Switch: an Ex-FBI Agent's Guide to Influencing, Attracting, and Winning People Over*. Simon & Schuster, 2015.

Wooden, John, and Jay Carty. *Coach Wooden's Pyramid of Success*. Regal, 2009.

Carnegie, Dale. *How to Win Friends & Influence People*. Simon & Shuster; Rev Sub Edition, 1981.

Keller, Gary. *The One Thing: the Surprisingly Simple Truth behind Extraordinary Results*. John Murray, 2014.

Duckworth, Angela. *Grit*. Vermilion, 2017.

.

31535556R00083

Printed in Great Britain
by Amazon